# OMG!

## How to Survive 101 of Life's Most F'ed Situations

Deborah Baer

adamsmedia
Avon, Massachusetts

Published by Adams Media,
a division of F+W Media, Inc.
57 Littlefield Street, Avon, MA 02322. U.S.A.
www.adamsmedia.com

ISBN 10: 1-4405-0207-2
ISBN 13: 978-1-4405-0207-1

Printed in the United States of America.

10  9  8  7  6  5  4  3

Library of Congress Cataloging-in-Publication Data is available from the publisher.

This publication is designed to provide accurate and authoritative information with
regard to the subject matter covered. It is sold with the understanding that the publisher is not engaged in rendering legal, accounting, or other professional advice.
If legal advice or other expert assistance is required, the services of a competent
professional person should be sought.
    —From a *Declaration of Principles* jointly adopted by a Committee of the
    American Bar Association and a Committee of Publishers and Associations

Many of the designations used by manufacturers and sellers to distinguish their product are claimed as trademarks. Where those designations appear in this book and
Adams Media was aware of a trademark claim, the designations have been printed
with initial capital letters.

Certain sections of this book deal with activities and devices that would be in violation
of various federal, state, and local laws if actually carried out or constructed. We do
not advocate the breaking of any law. This information is for entertainment purposes
only. We recommend that you contact your local law enforcement officials before
undertaking any project based upon any information obtained from this book. We
are not responsible for, nor do we assume any liability for, damages resulting from
the use of any information in this book.

*This book is available at quantity discounts for bulk purchases.*
*For information, please call 1-800-289-0963.*

To P—because this book will
always remind me of you.

# Discussion Topics for Book Clubs

Here are thought-provoking questions to think about as you read *OMG!*

1. Throughout the book, humor is used to counterbalance the f'ed situations we all face. Does it seem appropriate? Does it change your perception of the author or make you think she is tacky, cold-hearted, and psychologically disturbed?

2. Did the book affect you in a personal way, such as offending you or making you uncomfortable? Or did you enjoy reading about farting, pooping, and getting your period?

3. How did your relationship with God change as a result of reading *OMG!*?

4. Why does Edward insist on being married before he turns Bella into a vampire? Oh wait, that's a question for the

*Twilight* book club. Sorry, moving on . . . .

5. What kind of person would you recommend this book to? Hint: probably someone very disturbed, like Charles Manson.

6. Why do you think the title of this book is *OMG!* as opposed to *Holy Shit!* or *You Gotta Be Kidding Me!*?

7. What f'ed up situations do you remember most vividly from *OMG!*? Have they made you look at the world or your friends differently?

8. The author weaves the imagery of art throughout the book. How come funny pictures and drawings bring the f'ed up situations to life so good?

9. How does *OMG!* reflect the author's own pathetic life? Are there obvious influences? Is the book better because the author was able to draw from her own f'ed up miserable existence?

10. By the end of the book, do you feel better—or much, much worse—about your own life?

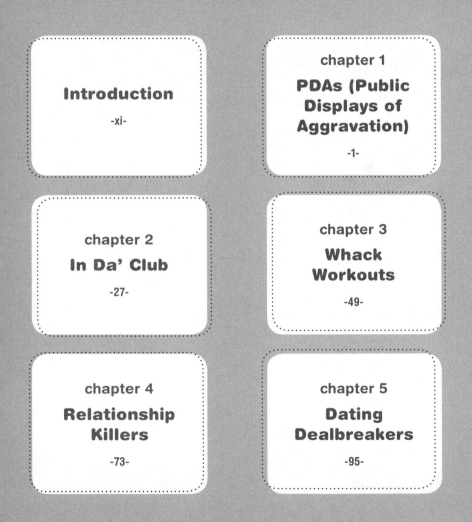

# Introduction

# What the F*#! Is OMG?

OMG! Does this sound familiar? Your boyfriend is posting pictures of his penis online, a bird pooped on your head, your boss has chronic halitosis, and some idiot spilled red wine on your white carpet. When life blows big chunks, you may just want to scream, "Oh my GOD!" at the top of your lungs (or "Oh my GOSH!" for all the Bible thumpers out there).

But saying the whole sentence is so 1993. In this age of technological wonder, you can rattle off three little letters, O-M-G, and it's totally therapeutic. It's understood universally that you are one of the following adjectives: shocked, awed, surprised, disgusted, flabbergasted, flummoxed, astounded, blown away, stunned, dazed, shaken, stirred, bewildered, angry...okay, that's enough of the computer thesaurus. You get the idea. You live it. You are confronted with OMG! situations every day.

But sometimes these events seem so overwhelming, you can't even deal. That's where we come in. We have compiled a list of 101 of the most aggravating and infuriating scenarios—but to appease the ADD freaks out there, have broken them up into ten wonderful, easy-to-read chapters that cover everything from dating dilemmas to online etiquette blunders. And like a high-priced shrink, we offer the advice and tools to handle them like a pro (and we don't mean like a hooker, you slut).

So inhale OMG! and let the wisdom soak into your brain. When you're done, we guarantee you will be the smartest, most evolved person on the planet. President Barack Obama will ask you for advice and you will be capable of settling the Palestinian-Israeli conflict. Every man will want you and every woman will want to be you. Actually, the women may want you, too. Prepare to be idolized, admired, and worshipped.

# chapter 1

# PDAs (Public Displays of Aggravation)

# >>1. The person next to you on an airplane opens a can of tuna

**A**s if it wasn't enough that those cheap bastards at the airlines took away our pillows, our blankets, and our dignity. Now they're making us pay $10 extra for their vile airplane food, which often comes in a "snack box" and includes delectable fare such as processed cheese spread and salmonella-laced peanut butter crackers. Because of this new development, many thrifty travelers have taken matters—and their appetites—into their own hands and have started bringing their own meals onto the aircraft. But people are gross and they eat revolting things. Like, bringing hella stinky cans of tuna onboard and opening them before the plane even takes off. And everybody has to sit in fish stink for five hours! So not cool. But you can turn this to your advantage.

## The OMG! solution to dealing with a dumb person who brings smelly food on an airplane

### → STEP #1: Find out the offender's name

Engage the rude, selfish passenger in conversation and make introductions. For the reason why, see Step #5.

### → STEP #2: Complain to a flight attendant

Assuming you didn't already have a meltdown when the flight attendant insisted your $800 Theory leather jacket be taken out of the overhead, rolled up into a ball, and put under your seat on top of peanut crumbs and shoe guck, it is possible to have her help you in a time of need. Press the button-thingy and when she comes over, embarrass the tuna offender in front of everyone.

### → STEP #3: Demand a seat change to First Class

Tell the flight attendant you're allergic to Thunnus Maccoyii (a fancy word for tuna), cats, and peanuts, and that if you don't move, your throat will close up and you will die. And then she will go to prison for negligent homi-cide and a bull-dyke named Bar-bara will claim her as her wife.

### → STEP #4: Drink yourself into a stupor on free champagne

Once firmly lodged in your gigantic, cushy, new seat in first class, get stinkin' drunk. You deserve it.

### → STEP #5: Send an anonymous letter to the Department of Homeland Security

Once on land, mail an anonymous letter to the government and tell them that the tuna lady, whose name you learned in Step #1, is a terrorist.

### OMGesus!

Want decent airplane food? You'll have to fly all the way to Chang-chun to eat it. According to Sky-trax, Asiana Airlines has the best economy class grub!

**Top 10 Flight Risks**

More things that should be banned on airplanes, besides tuna:

1. Taking off your shoes
2. Crop dusting (that's when flight attendants or passengers expel gas as they walk up and down the aisle)
3. Stinking up the bathroom, unless it's a true emergency
4. Cell phone reception
5. Pilots who use the intercom to practice their stand-up act
6. Parents who can't control their babies' screaming
7. Keeping the overhead light on if the person next to you is sleeping
8. People who board before their zone is called
9. Anyone with chronic halitosis
10. Business class passengers leaving their section in shambles—what a bunch of animals!

## >>> 2. A bird craps on your head

**Y**ou're on a hot date with a sexy guy, sitting outside along the ocean dining al fresco. He's about to feed you a chocolate-covered strawberry, when all of a sudden you feel a light thump on your head. A seagull just shit in your hair—and now the gooey excrement is about to drip down onto your face. You must act fast because that winged serpent not only just ruined your blowout, the man of your dreams is seconds away from doing the "Check, please!" signal.

## The OMG! solution for being totally humiliated by a bird with IBS

### →OPTION #1: Rattle off humorous birdshit factoids

To detract attention, impress your date with your knowledge of poop culture. For instance, according to an exhaustive Google search, Cyndi Lauper once had a bird poop in her mouth while she was singing. Another time, a sparrow dropped a bomb on former president George W. Bush while he sat in the Rose Garden.

### →OPTION #2: Rub it all over your face

It's the new hot trend in skin-care—nightingale droppings are reportedly the secret ingredient that keeps David and Victoria

"Posh" Beckham's perfect skin glowing! In New York City, the Shizuka Day Spa offers a $50 Geisha Facial that uses powdered bird dung.

## OMGesus!

According to a study done at the University of Tasmania, seagulls are getting so fat on greasy take-out garbage like French fries, high cholesterol is destroying their eggs—and their population is declining.

### → OPTION #3: Kill the bird

As long as your date isn't one of those metrosexuals, take the Charter Arms .38 "Pink Lady" Revolver out of your purse and shoot your new feathered friend right out of the sky. Then ask the restaurant to fry it up with some lemon, capers, and a splash of white wine.

## Is It Good Luck—Or Does It Just Suck?

In many cultures, it's considered good fortune for a bird to take a dump on your head. Here are some other birdbrained superstitions.

### Rain on your wedding day

*Obviously, someone made this up to pacify or appease a freaked-out Bridezilla a long time ago. Because dark clouds, puddles, and gale force winds on the most expensive, er, important day of your life is never a good thing.*

### Lucky pennies

*You get all excited when you see it sitting in the street, all filthy and lonely. But after you pick it up, you realize you can't buy a damn thing with it and you have about 187*

*more useless pieces of copper in a jar under your sink.*

### Stray eyelashes

*In order for your dreams to come true, you're supposed to take it gently off the cheek, put it on the end of your finger and blow it off into the wind. But maybe that wayward eyelash is really a sign of something more sinister, like conjunctivitis or blepharitis.*

### Rabbit's foot

*A poor cute little bunny got his foot chopped off. That's not lucky, it's satanic!*

# 3. A jerk holds up the line at 7-Eleven buying a million Lotto tickets

**A**ll you wanna do is buy a Blue Woo Hoo Vanilla Slurpee and some nachos. But when you get to the counter, some douchebag is rattling off numbers like a bingo caller—and there's no end in sight. OMG! Your nacho cheese is stiffening up like a corpse and your icy-cold drink is numbing your hand. Hurry up!

## The OMG! solution for speeding up the line

### → STEP #1: Give him statistics

Tell the guy he's wasting his money, that the likelihood of winning a Powerball is about 1 in 146 million. And according to Web-Math.com, he has a better chance of getting in a car accident, dying in a plane crash, or being struck by lightening than winning a lottery.

### → STEP #2: Sabotage him

If that doesn't sway him, start shouting out random numbers. Ten! Eleven! Seventeen! Twenty-three! Thirty-three! Thirty-five! It'll confuse the guy behind the counter. It'll be total anarchy!

## → STEP #3: Bring up feminine hygiene products

No guy enjoys that. Tell him you're getting your period, like right that minute, and if he doesn't let you pay for your snacks ASAP, you will ruin your pants and send him the dry-cleaning bill.

### OMGesus!

According to Slurpee Nation (*www.slurpee.com/nation*), the scientific name for BrainFreeze is *sphenopalatine ganglioneuralgia*. BTW, pressing your tongue on the roof of your mouth is an instant cure.

## → STEP #4: If all else fails, get his number

You know, just in case he actually wins and you want a diamond necklace, a Birkin bag, or a pair of Jimmy Choos.

### The Lottery Curse

People who win the jackpot have bad stuff happen to them. You'll feel better knowing these facts:

*After winning $20 million, Jeffrey Dampier was kidnapped and murdered by his sister-in-law.*

*After Jack Whittaker won a $315 million Powerball, 400 people sued him, he was drugged at a strip club, and his granddaughter died from a drug overdose.*

*Billy Bob Harrell killed himself after winning $37 million because his wife left him.*

*Evelyn Adams won the lottery twice, for a total of $5.4 million, but gambled or gave it all away. Today, she lives in a trailer.*

*After Bud Post won $16.2 million, his brother hired a hitman to kill him. Bad investments ate up the whole pot of gold and now he lives on food stamps.*

# >>> 4. You are mistaken for a prostitute

**Y**ou're standing on a street corner, minding your own business. Suddenly, a Ford Taurus rolls up next to you and a nerdy middle-aged businessman asks, "How much to lick the lollipop, sweetheart?" OMG! He thinks you're a hooker! Gross!

## The OMG! solution for avoiding being sold into sex slavery

### → STEP #1: Find out how much he's willing to pay

Just kidding. You're not really going to get paid to fornicate. But since he asked you first, he can't be a cop because that would be entrapment. So you might as well find out how much you're worth!

### → STEP #2: Tell him he's on *To Catch a Predator*

Yell, "Surprise!" and point to a storefront window. Let him know that this has all been caught on camera and will be on an NBC news special next week. Inform him that SWAT teams are waiting around the corner to drag him out of his car, throw him on the pavement face first, and cuff him. Then watch the sucker peel away.

### → STEP #3: Write down the license plate number

Contact the DMV to get his phone number. Then call his wife and ruin his life. Tell her he tried to pick you up for sex but you told him you had crabs.

## Hookers with a Heart of Gold

These famous women have all played streetwalkers, and since they are role models for young girls, it must be acceptable to be a prostitute:

### Julia Roberts

*In* Pretty Woman, *she got paid for having sex with Richard Gere, stayed in a fancy five-star hotel, and got to go for shopping sprees on Rodeo Drive. Sign us up!*

### Rebecca DeMornay

*In* Risky Business, *she got to do it with Tom Cruise. That seems like a good enough reason to be a hooker!*

### Nicole Kidman

*In* Moulin Rouge, *she plays Satine, a call girl who has a nasty cough, yet the undivided attention of two dudes, one rich and the other a tortured artist. It's nice to be loved.*

### Debra Messing

*Okay, she's not the prostitute, the guy is. In* The Wedding Date, *she hires a gigolo to take her to a wedding, but then of course, ends up falling in love with him. So it doesn't matter that he's a walking STD!*

### OMGesus!

Now, this is gross. A study by Sven-Axel Mansson of Malmo University in Sweden found that about 16 percent of men pay for sex in the U.S.!

# 5. A mechanic overcharges you because you have a vagina

**Y**ou haven't come a long way, baby. Women may fly planes, fight wars, play hockey, and hock loogies, but there are two things the fairer sex still hasn't conquered—become president of the United States of America and get a fair shake at an auto repair shop. Let's be honest, when a woman walks into a garage, the grease monkeys behind the counter have dollar signs in their eyes and malice in their hearts. They know that we usually have no idea what they're talking about, so we nod along like nincompoops while they tell us our flux capacitors are missing a widget and that'll be $920.

## The OMG! solution to being overcharged for car repairs

If you're going to be treated like a girl, act like one and use your wily ways to bring the price down.

### → OPTION #1: Flirt

Even if your mechanic has paint-stripping BO and looks like he dipped his fingernails in diarrhea, stare at his package and tell him his butt looks cute in that jump-suit. Chitchat about things guys love, like the UFC, *Battlestar Galactica*, and masturbating.

### → OPTION #2: Cry

Do not underestimate the power of tears. Chop up an onion before you walk in and recite a heart-wrenching monologue about how you're sleeping in your car—this car—because you lost your home in the mortgage crisis.

### → OPTION #3: Sleep with the owner or manager

It worked for Long Island Lolita Amy Fisher. She shagged married garage owner Joey Buttafuoco and he fixed her 1989 Dodge Daytona. To show her appreciation, Amy shot his wife Mary Jo in the face.

> ## OMGjesus!
>
> 90 percent of women feel that they're treated like crap in auto repair shops, according to a Car Care Council survey.

### → OPTION #4: Call your daddy

If the above fails, bring a male figure with you to the shop. If the presence of another guy doesn't make their knees buckle, you can at least ask your father to lend you the 920 bucks.

### → OPTION #5: Do it yourself

If your dad hates you or is sick of bailing you out of trouble, it's time for DIY (one-third of DIY car repairs are done by women, says the Automotive Aftermarket Industry Association!). Register to take automotive repair classes at a local technical school or community college, which has Automotive Service Excellence certification. Actually, it's not a bad career move. The Bureau of Labor Statistics forecasts that repair shops nationwide face an annual shortage of about 35,000 technicians through 2010 and the average salary is about $42,000, according to the National Automobile Dealers Association.

> ### Why didn't we think of that?
>
> Ladies Choice Autocare in Ontario, Canada, has 40 percent female mechanics, offers wireless access and spa services while you wait for your car, and sells jewelry along with auto parts. The $75 Sweetheart package includes a manicure, lube, oil & filter change, and a mini-detail for your car.

## >> 6. You're in charge of saving seats at the movie

I t's opening night of the new Vampire movie. You've been the responsible one. You ordered tickets online ahead of time for your group of besties. You picked everyone up on time and drove them to the theater. And how do they repay you? They make you guard the seats while they get popcorn and go to the bathroom. And now every jackass in the theater is gunning for your row of seats. Every five seconds, you have to shout, "They're taken!"

## The OMG! solution for holding seats at a movie theater

### → OPTION #1: Bring accessories

If you don't have enough coats and purses to make it across the seats, block the section off with crime-scene tape, which you can get online on sites that sell novelty crap and Halloween costumes. If people think someone was violently murdered in those seats, they're definitely not going to want to sit there. Look very concerned, scared, and sad.

### → OPTION #2: Be obnoxious

Take out your cell phone and start talking on it loudly and rapidly. Make it look like you're the kind of person who will be talking throughout the previews and the entire movie. Say to an invisible friend on the other end of the line, "OMG! I can't believe we got in! Robert Pattinson is SO dreamy! I'm going to totally scream every time I see his face!

I can't believe you can't be here because your grandmother is in the hospital! I will totally give you a-play-by-play!"

## → OPTION #3: Enlist a bodyguard

Look for a nerdy guy. Call him over, bat your eyelashes and ask him if he'll stand guard at the end of the row. Say "Pwetty pwease!" And tell him you have a boyfriend, but if he helps you, you have a sexy girl to set him up with (which will be the ugliest or most annoying friend in your group).

## → OPTION #4: Let them have it

Screw your ungrateful friends! Give in and let strangers take the seats. When your pals come back, shrug and say, "I tried. . . ." Your friends will be forced to sit in the front row, which is a fitting punishment for abandoning you.

## Crime & Punishment

If OMG! owned a movie theater, we'd have a secret jail in the basement where those who lack the proper movie-watching etiquette would be interrogated and disciplined.

| Offense | Penalty |
|---|---|
| Talking back to the characters | Hot peppers rubbed on mouth |
| Chair kicking | Kathy Bates bludgeons your feet like in Misery |
| Texting | Slow, painful fingernail removal |
| Screaming baby | Excessive tickling |
| Wrapper crinkling | Loud, constant playing of Susan Boyle's music |

### OMGesus!

According to TheDailyPlate.com, it would take twenty minutes of intensive beach volleyball play to burn off the calories from eating buttered popcorn at a movie theater.

# >>> 7. The only acceptable costume on Halloween is trampy

**A**s Tina Fey wrote in *Mean Girls*, "Halloween is the one day of the year when girls can dress like sluts and nobody can talk about them." Yes, it's October 31, when cleavage is required to resemble two giant gourds, skirts shall barely cover your hoo-ha, and fishnets are not optional. Meanwhile, men get to have all the fun and dress like the Octomom, Spider-Man, or a giant penis. Nevertheless, it is your duty as the fairer sex to look hot and make even the most inane costume look naughty. Don't let society down.

## The OMG! list of the sexiest Halloween costumes

→**OPTION #1: Nurse**

You should look sponge-bath-worthy and have a stethoscope hanging around your plunging neckline.

→**OPTION #2: Catholic School Girl**

It's a cliché but it works.

→**OPTION #3: A cat**

Whether you are Catwoman or just a tabby, throw on a leotard, stick a ball of fur on your ass and draw some whiskers on your face. Easy, just like you.

→**OPTION #4: Hooter's girl**

You'd never think of stepping foot in the place on any other day, but it's the most popular job on Halloween. Love those sheer nylons!

### → OPTION #5: Soldier

Some costume shops actually sell a ready-made outfit called "Major Flirt." Girls + guns = hot.

### → OPTION #6: French maid

Learn a few phrases before you step out, like "Tu as un super petit cul!" ("Your butt is very nice!") or "Je suis un chaud-lapin!" ("I am a sex maniac!").

### → OPTION #7: Osama Bin Laden

Just checking to see if you're still paying attention.

### → OPTION #8: Pirate wench

Ask all the guys you meet how long their plank is, aaargh!

### → OPTION #9: Cheerleader

Every guy wants to "date" a cheerleader!

### → OPTION #10: Belly dancer

On any other day, it's an important cultural tradition. On Halloween, it's dirty and nasty!

## OMGjesus!

According to the National Confectioners Association, candy corn was invented in the 1880s, is almost pure sugar, and only has 3.57 calories per piece. Perfect for the anorexics out there!

### Halloween's Most Horrifying Urban Legends

#### Razor apples

*Almost all tales of poisoned candy turn out to be hoaxes. Although in 1964, cranky Helen Pfeil did give kids insecticide, steel wool, and dog biscuits and was convicted of child endangerment. And, according to news reports, in 1974, little Timmy O'Bryan's father, nicknamed "The Candy Man," actually put cyanide in* his son's Pixy Stix to get insurance money. Timmy died!

### Black cats disappear

*According to an urban legend, animal shelters ban the adoption of black cats during this time of year, fearing they'll be tortured by satanists! Not (entirely) true, depends on the shelter.*

### Pedophiles are everywhere

*Not anymore. According to a 2008 article in the L.A. Times by Cynthia Dizikes, in some states, like Maryland, sex offenders are required to post an orange sign at their house saying "No candy," and must stay home, turn off the lights, and not answer the door. Louisiana law states that some perverts are not allowed to wear masks, and a Texas statute allows cops to round them up and detain them. Creepy!*

### Murder and mayhem

*Actually, satanic rituals are not the number one killer on Halloween—it's traffic. More than 200 people die each year after getting hit by cars. Bummer, dude.*

## >>> 8. You can't remember someone's name

**Y**ou walk into a party with a friend and are saying hi to all your peeps when you spot a familiar face across the room. But for the life of you, you have no idea what name goes with that familiar face. And now the familiar face is making a beeline for you. And when the familiar face comes up to you, she knows your name. And now you have to make introductions and holy crap, you are blanking. Gulp.

### The OMG! solution for faking your way out of an introduction

→ **STEP #1: Stall**

Fill up the awkward space with lots of chatter about nothing. Say, "Hey! OMG! I haven't seen you in so long! What have you been up to? Tell me everything!"

→ **STEP #2: Deflect**

As soon as there is a pause in the conversation, introduce the mysterious stranger to your friend (if you are alone, skip to Step #3). Say, "This is my friend Crystal." Hopefully, the stranger will then say her name back, like, "Hi, nice to meet you! I'm Julie Chen!" If she doesn't, go to Step #3.

## → STEP #3: Pretend you have a call

Shake your purse, like it's vibrating, and say, "Oh, that's my cell. Excuse me, I'll be right back." Then go outside where the smokers are and ask one of them who this person is. Smokers know everybody because they all gossip as they huddle together like panhandlers.

## → STEP #4: Re-approach

Once you know the name, go back inside, go right up to her and say, "Hey Julie Chen!" like you're BFFs so she never has any clue that you had no friggin' idea who she was four minutes before.

### Name-Remembering Tricks

1. Say the person's name back as soon as you are introduced. But don't be thinking about the fact that you are saying their name back instead of listening to their name.
2. Repeat it over and over again, like you have Tourette's.
3. Make an association. Like if the person's name is Brian, maybe he likes Raisin Bran cereal. Ask him. Or if the person's name is Mindy, maybe she has minty breath. Ask her to blow in your face and pray that she didn't eat garlic for dinner.
4. Get a tattoo. After you meet the person, go get inked. You'll never forget the name and the person will be forever indebted to you. Or will file a restraining order. That's memorable, too.

## Unforgettable—and Stupid—Celebrity Baby Names

Kal-El Cage (Nicolas Cage)

Bronx Mowgli (Pete Wentz and Ashlee Simpson)

Moxie Crimefighter (Penn Jillette)

Moses (Gwyneth Paltrow and Chris Martin)

Bob (Charlie Sheen)

Pilot Inspektor (Jason Lee)

Knox (Brad Pitt and Angelina Jolie)

### OMGesus!

In Germany, parents can't just pick any old name for their bouncing bundles of joy. They must have the moniker approved by an office called the Standesamt. Recently rejected names include Whoopi, Hitler, and Osama.

# >> 9. A dog keeps sniffing your crotch

It's that time of the month again, and you feel like a harpooned whale, but you still want to go to your friend's party. You walk in and immediately your pal's pooch sticks his nose in your coochie. The record player scratches to a stop and everyone, including your crush, is staring. Now they all know that you are menstruating and bloated and bitchy. Terrific.

## The OMG! solution for gracefully getting a dog away from your vagina

### → OPTION #1: Make a joke

Say, "I must be a terrorist because there's a bomb in my pants!" or "Hey, I don't sniff on the first date!"

### OMGesus!

According to the DogAcademy.com, canines have super-strong noses with more than 220 million scent receptors. So if you're stanky, they gonna know it!

### → OPTION #2: Bend over

Instead of trying to push the dog's nose away every two seconds, get down to the dog's level immediately and start petting it. Whisper in its ear that you will never forget this and will ruin him one day.

### → OPTION #3: Let the dog sniff your hand

It's normal for a dog to smell your privates because he is attracted to the pheromones. But if you let him smell your hand, he'll get the same thing and may leave your magic carpet alone.

*In the Future...*

**Embarrassing Va-jay-jay Smells:** In another study, 10 percent of women admitted using products to combat vaginal odor. See your doctor if your vagina smells like Bud Light, coffee, or Gummy Worms because booze, caffeine, and sugar make for stinkier tunnels of love.

**The Best Synonyms for Vagina**

Cooter

Beaver

Shag carpet

Pink taco

Bearded clam

Honey pot

Beef curtain

# 10. A masseuse turns you on

**W**ho doesn't love getting a massage? It's so relaxing and peaceful, lying there listening to Enya while a complete stranger manhandles your body. Okay, let's be honest. Some of you are kind of weirded out about an unfamiliar person touching you so intimately. And even more of you are uncomfy taking off your undies and being totally naked under that sheet. So you might be a little freaked out when Olga's strong man-hands rub your butt in an excitement-inducing circular motion. Or when her powerful paws wander up your inner thigh, a little too close to your lady parts! But are you just being paranoid? This is a professional!

## The OMG! solution for avoiding a happy ending

### → STEP #1: Don't speak

You don't want your massage therapist to get the wrong idea. So don't say things like, "Oh yeah, mama, that feels good. Right there. That's the spot. You really know how to use your hands."

### → STEP #2: Do not moan

Instead of writhing with pleasure, think about unsexy things, like Dick Cheney, parallel parking, or bunions.

### → STEP #3: Burp

Every time the masseuse touches a sensitive area, belch. Then say, "Excuse me! I had Taco Bell for lunch." If you're really worried that she's going to go for it, you could expel gas when she kneads your butt. But that's a little extreme and only to be used in emergencies.

## OMGjesus!

Kevin Costner was once accused of exposing himself to a masseuse —on his honeymoon!

### The Naked Truth

- 80 percent of women don't like to look at themselves naked in the mirror, according to a poll in British *Marie Claire*.
- 79 percent of women have reservations about showering or changing in front of other women in the locker room, according to a survey by bathroom equipment company SHUC.
- 33 percent of women are embarrassed to be naked in front of a boyfriend or partner, let alone a complete stranger, the SHUC poll says.
- 10 percent of women disrobe in the dark, the same study found.

# chapter 2

# In Da'
# Club

# >> 11. The line to get in is a mile long

**Y**ou slip on your slinkiest dress, tease your hair up to the heavens, and head to the hottest new club in town. But when you get there, there are 100 other chicks that look exactly like you—and you're not on the VIP list. The bouncer is big and mean, and he's so ugly, sexual favors are definitely not an option.

## The OMG! solution for weaseling your way past the velvet rope

### → OPTION #1: Act like you work there

Try to remember the DJ's name from that flyer. Walk causally up to the bouncer alone, like you don't give a shit about anything (perhaps while even listening to your iPod). Then inform him that you're one of the DJ's cage dancers. Or, you can say you're the club's new cigarette girl. Or one of those big-boobed girls who walk around giving shots to people out of test tubes.

### → OPTION #2: Pretend you're connected

Tell the bouncer you're meeting your boyfriend, Junior Gotti, and his best friend, A.J. Soprano, inside and if you're even one minute late, Carmine will put cement blocks on his ankles and throw him into the river.

### → OPTION #3: Name drop

Say that you're the publicist for some C-list star, like Tori Spelling or Kim Kardashian, and that you have to get inside to set up bottle service for her VIP table.

### → OPTION #4: Appeal to his sensitive side

Most if not all bouncers are jaded and cynical and have heard every excuse in the book. But have they ever granted a dying wish? Not likely! Tell him you're with the Make-A-Dream-Come-True foundation and you only have three months to live. And happily dancing the night away at this club is #1 on your Bucket List.

### → OPTION #5: Pay

You could slip him a twenty spot but that's so unimaginative, and could buy at least one cocktail! You also run the risk of him keeping it—and still not letting you in. Evil bastard.

#### Pathetic Pickup Lines

Guys who have read *The Game* or watched that stupid reality TV show *The Pick-Up Artist* may try to use these openings, called "gambits," as ice-breakers. But because of OMG!, you'll recognize them immediately and know that the guy has absolutely no game because he has to rely on the teachings of a goggle-wearing, effeminate weirdo named Mystery.

- "Did you see the fight outside?"
- "What movie is this from? 'Nobody puts Baby in a corner!'"
- "Let me ask you a question: Do you think it's cheating if you have a boyfriend but kiss someone else when you're drunk?"
- "Do you floss before or after you brush?"

### OMGesus!

A study on the psychology of queuing in the *Journal of Consumer Research* has found that people who know ahead of time how long they will have to wait in line freak out less than those who don't have a clue.

# >> 12. You don't have money for drinks

**W**ith the economy in the toilet, you're broke—and guys are even more stingy than normal about buying a thirsty lady a damn drink. But it's essential you get your cocktail on, so the night isn't a total waste. And please, it's not as much fun to dance sober. So, what's a cash-strapped gal to do?

## The OMG! solution for mooching free booze

### →OPTION #1: Beg

In a ladylike way, of course. Find your mark—e.g, an ugly, lonely man wearing an expensive watch. Tell him you really admire his stimulus package. And watch how fast you have a drink in hand. Stick with your mark for as long as it takes you to get drunk—or until he feels he has the right to grab your boob. Once he crosses the line, tell him you have to pee, then disappear into the crowd.

### →OPTION #2: Borrow

Ask the one friend in your group who's a total doormat to lend you money for a drink. Because that friend is such a people pleaser and has such low self-esteem, she will open a tab and let you drink on it all night long.

### →OPTION #3: Steal

If all else fails, when nobody is looking, drink the half-empties sitting up on the bar or on tables temporarily vacated for dancing/

smoke breaks. Just pretend that you genuinely believe that drink is yours—and make sure you don't accidentally pick up a tobacco spittoon cup or something.

### → OPTION #4: Bring your own

It's totally ghetto, but you could bring your own flask or slip some bottles in under your coat or in your hair extensions.

## WHAT YOUR DRINK SAYS ABOUT YOU

| DRINK | YOU |
| --- | --- |
| Bud Light | One of the guys |
| Guinness | Butch lesbian |
| Cosmo/Stoli cranberry | Slutty sorority girl |
| Whiskey/Rum/Gin | Seriously troubled and on your way to losing your teeth and living in a trailer park |
| White Zinfandel | Bridge & Tunnel* |
| Red Bull & vodka | Life of the party |
| Mojito | High-maintenance |
| Martini | Snob |

* Refers to the outer-borough peasants who invade their local city on weekends

# >>> 13. A guy tries to get you wasted

There are a lot of horny toads out there, especially at clubs, who may try to ply you with drinks in order to more easily convince you to go home with him. Mr. Perv always seems to know when your glass is empty and either tops yours off or always has another drink on the ready. If you're a lush, this can be enticing. But you must be aware at all times that this guy has an ulterior motive—getting you so plastered you'd even go home with Clay Aiken.

## The OMG! solution for avoiding drunken hookups with losers

### → OPTION #1: Superglue your glass to your hand

That's right. That way, you'll always know how much you have left, and can avoid refills and roofies. And then you'll also never be parched, even when you go to the loo, smoke a joint in the alley, or do the white man's overbite on the dance floor.

### → OPTION #2: Pass it off

Look, you don't want to turn down free booze (see #12). But you also don't want to get pregnant or contract an STD. So any time a guy buys you a drink, give it to your poorest and ugliest pal. She'll be grateful and you won't be vulnerable!

## → OPTION #3: Pour it in a plant

When he's not looking, dump it. They do that in the movies all the time.

## → OPTION #4: Do it to him

Start buying the jerk drinks, too, so that he gets so snockered, he passes out instead of making passes at you!

## → OPTION #5: Puke

Right on his shoes. He probably won't find you all that attractive anymore and will leave you alone.

### OMGjesus!

In the future, be wary of creepy dudes. And keep a ledger. According to researchers, up to 4 percent of the male population are sociopaths. So if you've been out about ninety-six times, and nothing weird's happened, the next four guys will probably try to roofie you. Watch your back! And your front!

### How to Spot a Sociopath

- He has no conscience. He might talk about killing kittens or ask the DJ to play a Josh Groban tune.
- He has no ability to feel shame. He might have a cubic zirconium diamond earring or wear those ugly football sweatpants with zig-zag patterns.
- He shows no guilt or remorse. Perhaps he'll eat all of the popcorn in the bowl on the bar and not offer you any.
- He has delusions of grandeur. He might tell you that he's a movie producer or a close personal friend of Adolf Hitler. But you'll know he's lying because Adolf Hitler is dead.

# 14. A trashy ho' threatens to scratch your eyes out

So, you're on the dance floor, practicing your best Crank Dat moves, when you accidentally step on a foot. But it's not just any foot. It belongs to a ginormous angry skank, who has vocal cords destroyed by White Zinfandel and long brown cigarettes, and pointy fake fingernails that should be registered as lethal weapons. After lots of screaming, talk-to-the-hand waves, and head-bobbing, she gathers her menacing posse around her and wants to take it outside. Problem is, you are a sissy.

## The OMG! solution to avoiding a girl-fight

### → OPTION #1: Take off your clothes

It will end the fight immediately. First, the guys in the club will start hooting and hollering and immediately come to your defense. Second, nobody wants to fight a naked person, with his or her private parts wiggling all over the place. Third, you'll probably get kicked out, arrested or sent to the loony bin, which, in the long run, may be better than having your pretty face rearranged.

### → OPTION #2: Challenge her to a dance-off

Yell, "Hit it!" to the DJ. He'll put on Michael Jackson's "Bad," your wingwomen can tie knives onto one of your hands, while you both grasp each other's free hand. Then you'll spin around in circles and slash the air furiously.

### → OPTION #3: Laugh it off

Play the humor card and tell some self-deprecating jokes. Say something like, "Are these my shoes or the boxes they came in?" How about, "I'm so uncoordinated, I throw a rock at the ground and miss!" Or, "I'm so stupid, I had to call 411 to get the number for 911!"

### → OPTION #4: Run

All of that hard work on the treadmill will now pay off. Just like geometry, sprinting is one of those skills that are essential to learn but rarely utilized. Kick off your Louboutins (of course, make sure one of your friends stays behind to pick them up) and make a mad dash for the exit.

### Famous Catfights in History

#### Alexis vs. Krystle (1981 to 1989)

*The Dynasty socialites had at least three knock-down drag-out fights, with face slapping, thrown vases, dress ripping, choking with pink feather boas, rolling around on the ground, and hurled insults such as "You crazy cow!" In one classic brawl, Alexis and Krystle end up in a lily pond and try to drown each other.*

#### Jane vs. Sydney (circa 1995)

*After Sydney steals Jane's husband Michael then prances around in their grandmother's wedding dress, the Melrose Place sisters throw each other into the pool. Jane calls Sydney "The Bride of Frankenstein."*

#### Teri vs. Charlize (1996)

*In the movie Two Days in the Valley, when Charlize Theron's character calls Teri Hatcher's character "a little bitch" all hell breaks loose. Teri gives her a right hook and a kick to the stomach, Charlize throws*

Teri over two tables, Teri smashes a glass on Charlize's face and gives her a couple of roundhouse kicks to the head. Good stuff.

### Pumpkin vs. New York (2007)

*On the VH1 reality show* Flavor of Love, *when Pumpkin is eliminated by Flavor Flav, she spits in fellow contestant New York's face, who responds with hair pulling and a hefty push to the pavement.*

### Danica vs. Milka (2008)

*NASCAR champ Danica Patrick gets pissed when Milka Duno blocks her path at the Honda Indy 200. When Patrick confronts her female rival in the pit, Duno throws a towel in her face—twice.*

### Sharon vs. Megan (2009)

*On the* Rock of Love: Charm School *reunion show, Sharon Osbourne, 50, goes postal on bikini-clad student Megan Hauserman, 26, when she calls Sharon's husband Ozzy "a brain-dead rock star." Sharon calmly takes a sip of water, then launches across the stage and rips Megan's head off.*

## OMGesus!

According to the FBI, girls' arrests for assault shot up 40.9 percent from 1992 to 2003, while boys' rose just 4.3 percent.

# 15. A Guido grinds against you on the dance floor

C an't a girl just lose herself in the music without being man-handled by every tool in the club? God forbid you make out with your best friend or caress her breasts when Lady GaGa comes on. It's like every guy thinks that's an invitation to join in on the action. Then the slimeball glides up, presses his crotch between your cheeks and grinds away. And all you're thinking is, Go away!

## The OMG! solution to fending off unwanted advances on the dance floor

### →OPTION #1: Tell the Guido you have diarrhea

Ask him to stop grinding because your ass is still burning from the explosive, watery dump you took after eating Indian food earlier that night. No guy wants to picture a hot girl pooping, so that should send him on his way.

### →OPTION #2: Dance really bad

Start flailing around like Elaine on *Seinfeld*. Just go totally off beat, with wild arms and kicks all over the place. Embarrass yourself so that people laugh at you. He will laugh at you—then leave you alone because you are suddenly very unsexy.

### → OPTION #3: Make out with a big guy

Pick the biggest baddest dude you can find. It will scare away any wimpy cheeseballs.

### → OPTION #4: Pretend to have a seizure

In this case, your tongue rolling around and your eyes rolling into to the back of your head isn't ecstasy, it's a medical emergency.

### OMGesus!

70 percent of women have intentionally given out the wrong telephone number, according to SoSuave.com.

# >>> 16. A drunken frat boy calls you "fat"

**Y**ou spent hours picking out the perfect outfit so you can shake your booty. You even took Polaroids of yourself to make sure you look hot and sexy. But after you turn down a drink from an annoying frat boy wearing a button-down polo and a backwards baseball hat, your already fragile self-esteem is crushed into pieces. As you walk away, he says loud enough for all to hear, "I'd never nail that whale anyway."

## The OMG! solution to handling a fat joke—about you

→ **OPTION #1: Channel George Costanza**

Say, "The jerk store called. They're running out of you!" And then all of the *Seinfeld* fans will laugh at him instead of you.

→ **OPTION #2: Tell him you slept with his girlfriend**

And then inform him that the girlfriend complained that he has a small penis.

→ **OPTION #3: Make him feel bad**

Tell him you have a thyroid condition like Oprah and that without medication and cupcakes, you will slip into a coma.

→ **OPTION #4: Get spiritual**

Tell him this story about Buddha: One day a rude person came up to Buddha and said, "Yo, who died and made you boss? You're a phony." And Buddha goes, "If you buy a gift for someone, and that person does not take it, who does the gift belong to?" And the guy goes, "Me, because I bought it." So Buddha goes, "Right. And it is exactly the same with your anger. If you become angry with me and I do not get insulted, then the anger falls back on you. You are the only one who becomes unhappy. All you have done is hurt yourself." He'll be so confused that he'll bro hug you.

### → OPTION #5: Throw your drink in his face and slap him

If he's an agnostic or an atheist, and reasoning with his morality doesn't work, go all old-school on him. It's justifiable and if it went to trial, no doubt you will have a sympathetic jury.

## OMGesus!

About 55 percent of normal-weight girls think they are too fat, according to a study by the American Dietetic Association.

### Best "Yo Mama" Jokes

If all else fails, insult the jerk-store's mother. Here are the best zingers, from AhaJokes.com:

1. Yo mama so fat, she was lying on the beach and everyone was running around shouting "Free Willy!"
2. Yo mama so fat that when she wears a yellow raincoat, people shout "Taxi!"
3. Yo mama so fat she got her own area code!
4. Yo mama so fat, every time she walks in high heels, she strikes oil!
5. Yo mama so fat, she broke her leg and gravy fell out!

## 17. You have to pee and a couple is having sex in the only bathroom stall

There's nothing worse than slamming back a bunch of cocktails and then realizing it will take forty-five minutes to stand in line for the filthy, urine-soaked bathroom. Even worse are the clubs where there are unisex stalls and either several girls are snorting something in there or a horny hookup is holding everyone up. When expletives and pounding on the door just doesn't work, here are some other options to avoid a big, bad bladder explosion.

## The OMG! solution to avoid peeing in your pants

### → OPTION #1: Video and blackmail them

A good sex tape can earn you thousands, if not millions, of dollars! Just ask Paris Hilton, Pamela Anderson, Kim Kardashian, and Screech.

### To Sit or Not to Sit . . .

"Fifty percent of American women won't sit on a seat without some type of guard or without hovering," Allison Janse, author of *The Germ Freak's Guide to Outwitting Colds and Flu*, told *20/20*. But in a test, it was the cleanest thing in the ladies' room—actually, the sanitary napkin disposal unit had the most germs. Ewwww.

## OMGesus!

95 percent of men and women claim that they wash their hands after using a public toilet, but researchers from the American Society of Microbiology (ASM) have discovered that only 67 percent actually do.

→ **OPTION #2: Tell them you're calling their parents**

Nobody wants to hear about their mom or dad when they are having sex. That should make the dude's wee-wee deflate in no time.

→ **OPTION #3: Join in**

Hey, some people are really into golden showers.

### Words of Wisdom

"To my knowledge, no one has ever acquired an STD on the toilet seat—unless they were having sex on the toilet seat," Abigail Salyers, PhD, president of the ASM, told WebMD.com.

### More Dumb Places to Boink

Couples have been arrested for having public sex in these strange spots:

**1. On train tracks**
A couple in South Africa was reportedly run over after insisting on finishing the deed.

**2. On a cop car**
A couple from Denmark did it on the roof of the patrol car as the officers sat inside their car.

**3. On a crane**
A Florida pair was living life on the edge when they did the horizontal mambo at the top of the construction apparatus.

**4. In a cockpit**
Southwest Airlines once fired two male pilots for flying their plane naked.

**5. In a graveyard**
A French couple made their own porno on hallowed ground. Lovely.

# 18. A hot guy wants to take you home, but you didn't shave

**Y**ou pick up the cutest guy in the club and after making out and fondling each other in a dark corner, he seductively whispers the magic words in your ear: "Let's get out of here." Here's the rub. You were going to stay home and watch *Golden Girls* re-runs on Lifetime but at the last minute, your friend convinced you to come out. Unfortunately, in your haste, you didn't have a chance to weed the garden.

## The OMG! solution to hooking up when you're hairy

### → OPTION #1: Adopt a European persona

Since you've been busy playing tonsil hockey, maybe he didn't notice your Long Island dialect. If he didn't, immediately start talking in, like, a fake Bosnian or Polish accent. Because everyone knows the chicks across the pond don't shave. They've got hairy pits and legs and giant afros between their legs. This way, if and when he sees you naked, he will not be shocked. If he is, tell him you're flying back to Romania early in the morning and have to go. And hope you never see him again.

### → OPTION #2: Be honest

Just flat out tell him he can get lucky but your legs might be a little prickly. Chances are pretty good that he'll suck it up and choose getting some action, instead of going home alone and bopping the baloney.

## OMGesus!

According to a study by Vagisil, 9 percent of women shave it all off "down there." Not surprisingly, 14 percent of women are so totally weirded out even saying the word "vagina" that they'd rather say "down there."

### → OPTION #3: Keep your pants on

Don't be a slut! Why is that so hard for you?

### In Other News:

Researchers in England believe that women are more attracted to men with stubbly chins than men who are clean shaven or have full beards.

### Famous Hairy Beasts

Look, just because these celebrities don't shave doesn't mean you shouldn't!

**Julia Roberts** *is supposed to be a Pretty Woman, but she looked more like a Canadian lumberjack at the 1999 premiere of* Notting Hill *when her fuzzy underarms caused quite a stir. At the time, she was dating Benjamin Bratt, who apparently found it a "turn on."*

**Drew Barrymore** *stunned the fashion world when she showed up to a Marc Jacobs show in 1995 with hairy pits.*

**Beyonce's** *underarm region resembled a collection of pubes at the Cadillac Records premiere in 2008.*

**Britney Spears** *has been seen out in tank tops with straggly hairs emerging from her pits. But then again, she once checked into a mental hospital, so . . . .*

# >>> 19. Your friends want to go to a strip club

**Y**our idea of a good time is not watching silicone-enhanced Barbie dolls slither around a pole and bounce their butts up and down in your lap. However, your guy friends and more liberal-minded girlfriends have all bought into this whole filthy mainstreaming of porn culture. So they drag you to the local jiggle joint, called something like Sugar and Spice, and after forking over a $20 cover, you enter the mammary Mecca and beg God for forgiveness.

## The OMG solution to surviving a strip club

### →STEP #1: Get a drink

You'll need to loosen up, so head to the bar for a $15 beer. Ask the bartender for singles so you can stick the dollar bills between the exotic dancers' butt cheeks.

### →STEP #2: Buy a lap dance

When in Rome . . . find the sweetest-looking girl and summon her over. Give her twenty bucks but tell her you don't want a lap dance, you just want to talk. Ask her real name, because they love that, and ask her where she's from and how she ended up taking off her clothes for a living.

### →STEP #3: Preach

Once you've gained her trust, convince her that this is not a respectable way to make a living and that she should love and respect her body, which is her temple. When she explains that stripping is empowering, make a sad scrunchy face and say, "No, it really isn't." Offer her a tissue when she begins to cry.

### → STEP #4: Organize a walk-out

Tell her to go to the dressing room, gather up her rip-away dresses, skanky stilettos, and drugged out coworkers, and run for the exits.

## OMGesus!

An actual study by University at Albany showed that male strippers get into the profession because they like showing off their bodies. Male dancers (75 percent) are more likely to date a customer than female dancers (only 21 percent). But 89 percent of female dancers would recommend dancing to a friend. Hey, like a dentist recommending Dentyne!

### → STEP #5: Start a riot

As the girls flee, flip over the tables, run into the DJ booth, grab the microphone and chant, "Women's liberation gonna smash that cage! Come join us now and rage, rage, rage!"

### → STEP #6: Don't bend over for the soap

Because you're probably going to jail.

## 20. Your wasted BFF is about to leave with a walking STD

**Y**our friend got trashed before you even got to the club. Once you walked in the door, she immediately went MIA. At one point you saw her making out with an Iraq vet in the corner (good for her, she's supporting our troops!). But then you saw her playing tonsil hockey with a guy who looked like he was fifteen. And yet an hour later, she told you she was leaving with the club playa—the guy who's hooked up with practically every girl on the planet. You must stop her before she ends up with crabs or something.

### The OMG solution for saving a drunk friend from making a horrible mistake

→ **OPTION #1: Make a list**

Okay, she's drunk, so it will be harder to get through to her. Grab a cocktail napkin and quickly write down the names of every girl who has ever left with this guy. Pull her aside and read it aloud to her. When you get to the end of the list, start over without

> "I'm not the type of guy who enjoys one-night stands. It leaves me feeling very empty and cynical. It's not even fun sexually."
>
> —BEN AFFLECK

stopping. It'll sound like a lot of girls and she's so hammered she won't remember the names you've already rattled off. As a bonus, after the second run through, say her name and ask "Do you really want to join the slut cycle?"

## → OPTION #2: Flash forward to the self-loathing

Remind her that studies show that while 80 percent of men feel great the next day, only 54 percent of women had positive feelings about a quickie with a stranger, while the others reported feeling "cheap" and "used."

## → OPTION #3: Go with her

Insist on being the third wheel. The guy will get annoyed that you are there and bolt.

## → OPTION #4: Buy him a hooker

Surely there's a lady of the night trolling around the bar. Pool your friends' money, slip her some cash, and hopefully she can steer the player away from your pal.

*In the Future...*

Ask a potential mate if they have any of these STD symptoms before getting naked with them:

- Painful urination
- Gray, white, green, or yellow discharge
- Sore testicles
- Rectal infections
- Warts

## OMGjesus!

Man, we sure do have low self-esteem! Women have one-night stands because they are flattered to be wanted—but men see themselves as lowering their standards to have a one-time fling, researchers at Durham University in England found.

# chapter 3

# Whack Workouts

OMG!

# >> 21. You fart during yoga class

You're in a zone, in the midst of a plow pose, when suddenly a sonic boom is released from your rear end. You are totally mortified and humiliated. Fortunately, you're probably not alone. Farting during yoga class is quite common, because the body movements are increasing blood flow to your digestive organs. But a science lecture doesn't come in handy when you're in the moment—especially when you've just ripped one in your teacher's face after she gently pressed down on your lower back. Oops.

## The OMG! solution to tooting in public

### → OPTION #1: Ignore it

Even if everyone around you giggles, stay focused and in a Zen-like state. Your seriousness about yoga and spirituality will make everyone else feel bad about being so childish and immature.

### → OPTION #2: Go with it

Cry out "Hey, did somebody step on a duck?" or "It was the Uka-tasana" (which means "chair" in Sanskrit). And then fart again for good measure.

### → OPTION #3: Blame it on someone else

Look at the person next to you and shake your head disapprovingly. For dramatic effect, wave your hand in front of your nose and pull your shirt up over your mouth and nose.

### → OPTION #4: Cover it up

Make other noises, like coughing or rubbing your foot on the rubber mat, so people aren't sure what they heard.

## OMGesus!

According to Dr. Fart, AKA The King of Gas (who, per an article on Salon.com, was a gastroenterologist and associate chief of staff at the Minneapolis Veterans Affairs Medical Center), everybody toots. Healthy people fart ten to twenty times a day—that's about a half a liter.

# In the Future...

## 1. Watch what you eat

According to Work of Heart Yoga (http://workofheartyoga.com), don't snack up to two hours before class, especially protein. Don't eat corn, cauliflower, cabbage, milk, bread, beer (probably not a good idea anyway), or raisins. To control excessive farting, try Artichoke Leaf Extract supplements, which supposedly help digestion. And go to the bathroom before class.

## 2. Wear fart-protective clothing

In 2007, a company called Undertec designed a diaper-like apparatus called Fartypants, which prevents gases from escaping. "They can be worn anytime, anywhere—in bed, to work, at social events, including professional meetings or when traveling in any vehicle, including an airplane," spokesman Buck Weimer said in a press release.

## 3. Avoid certain poses

If you've had beans for lunch, you may want to skip certain gas-inducing poses, such as Dhanurasa (Bow Pose), Jathara Parivartana-san (reclined twist), Marichyasan (seated twist), and Malasan (squats). Also, moves like the Vajrasana and Pawanmuktasa were designed to properly position the sphincter and help digestion. So just clench those cheeks extra tight when you know those are coming up.

# 22. The person before you didn't wipe off the handlebars

**A** fat, hairy guy is hogging the elliptical. Finally, when his time is up, he gets off—but instead of cleaning up his stinky sweat, he saunters away without a care in the world. Grody to the max.

## The OMG! solution to confronting a gym pig

→ **STEP #1:** Get a towel and soak up his revolting puddle of man juice.

→ **STEP #2:** Find the gym pig. Hopefully he is bending over and can't see you.

→ **STEP #3:** Twirl up the towel and snap his ass with the sharpest point.

→ **STEP #4:** When he turns around, smother his face in the sweat-drenched towel.

→ **STEP #5:** Wring the wet towel and leftover drippings on his head.

→ **STEP #6:** Walk straight to the office and lodge a complaint.

### OMGesus!

According to numerous news reports, as he ran on a treadmill, Wall Street villain Richard Fuld, CEO of bankrupt Lehman Brothers during the recession, was punched in the face and knocked out cold by an angry employee.

**Top 5 Gym Etiquette Faux Pas**

1. Hogging the machines

2. If you're a man, wearing short shorts

3. Dropping weights

4. Making inappropriate pelvic thrusts

5. Blasting your iPod

| **OMG!** > The person before you didn't wipe off the handlebars

# >>> 23. A lesbian watches you undress

There's an honor code in the locker room. Although it's very hard to avoid looking at the old women with their giant, saggy boobs and bathing caps, it is a rule of thumb that you don't compare and contrast the other naked bodies all around you. Which is why it's quite awkward when that cooty connoisseur who looks like a fourteen-year-old boy keeps staring at you when you come out of the shower and put silky lotion all over your hot, supple body.

## The OMG! solution to fending off the advances of a rug-muncher at the gym

### → OPTION #1: Lobby Congress

Is it fair that these Friends of Martina are allowed in the same locker room? Don't think so! That's like putting a hungry snake and a rat in the same cage. The rat must be protected! Vagitarians should legally be required to undress in separate accommodations at the gym, where they can talk about field hockey and Brandi Carlile. Call your local senator ASAP.

### → OPTION #2: Announce that you are looking for a sugar mama

Lesbians are notoriously cheap (and bad tippers, FYI). Once the boi senses you're a gold digger, her eyes will grow cold and she'll find a new target. (A "boi" is a young boyish-looking lezzie.)

> "I'm not gay, but I'll learn."
>
> —HOMER SIMPSON

### → OPTION #3: Talk about your BFF Miss California

The Miss America contestant publicly dissed gay marriage at the 2009 pageant and stuck to her platform even after Perez Hilton declared her a "dumb bitch." Since you are pretending to be pals with Miss California, the lesbian will have no choice but to find you abhorrent.

## OMGesus!

54 percent of women between the ages of eighteen and twenty-four have kissed another woman, according to a Cosmo poll.

### → OPTION #4: Say you hate the environment

Yes, that's right—lezzies are all pretty PC. So if you insist that global warming gives you a good tan and that you hate recycling, she'll stop bothering you. Also, talk about your new giant SUV and how you like buying bottled water every day and leaving the lights on because you get scared of the Boogie Monster.

**Hottest lesbian action!**

Maybe you want to hook up with a lesbian. If so, learn how by watching these famous movie scenes.

- Scarlett Johansson and Penelope Cruz, two of the most gorgeous women on the planet, are in love with the same man but make sweet love together anyway in *Vicky Christina Barcelona*.
- Angelina look-alike Megan Fox and *Mama Mia!* star Amanda Seyfried lock lips in the horror flick *Jennifer's Body*.
- Kelly McGillis and Jodie Foster were rumored to have had an affair while filming *The Accused*. And while the movie is about rape, there is some serious chemistry between these two ladies, who play lawyer and client. P.S.: Jodie Foster is still locked in the closet, but Kelly McGillis finally came out in April 2009.
- Denise Richards and Neve Campbell in *Wild Things*. Technically it's a ménage with Matt Dillon, but nobody's watching him anyway!

# >> 24. Someone catches you peeing in the shower

**Y**ou step in a stall, all sweaty and tight from a great workout. But as soon as the warm water cascades down your back, you loosen up and get a warm tingly feeling in your loins. The next thing you know, your wee-wee is going down the drain. Unfortunately, as you're standing there like a modern-day Venus statue, the curtain opens and another gym member witnesses your fountain of tinkle. Oops.

## The OMG! best excuses when you've been caught piddling

### → OPTION #1: You've been bitten by a jellyfish

Everyone thinks that urine helps relieve the sting. Even though it's actually not scientifically true, tell her there's a jellyfish in the pipes and to go get help immediately! Then run away naked.

### → OPTION #2: You have athlete's foot

Madonna famously declared on the David Letterman show in the '90s that peeing on your feet can cure fungus. Again, totally not true, but unless the infuriated stranger is a scientist from Stanford, you're pretty safe.

### → OPTION #3: You were thirsty

Tell the gym officials you are a practitioner of "urine therapy," which basically means you drink your own pee-pee, and you needed to quench your thirst because you were parched from yoga class. Mention that Jim Morrison and Paul McCartney were reportedly practitioners of urine therapy.

### → OPTION #4: You are incontinent

Millions of women accidentally pee when they cough, laugh, or run. You just ran like five miles. Tell anyone who cares that they're lucky you peed here instead of on the treadmill.

### → OPTION #5: You are a drug addict

You could say that you are late to a meeting with your probation officer and needed a sample—and could someone hand you a glass?

### *Celebrities Do It, Too*

*American Idol* champ Kelly Clarkson admits she pees in the shower and told *Blender* magazine, "Anybody who says they don't is lying."

### Taking the Piss

- In ancient Rome, people used urine to whiten their teeth.
- In France in the old days, people used to put urine-soaked stockings around their necks to cure strep throat.
- In China, babies' faces were once scrubbed with urine to protect their skin.

# >>> 25. You have a crush on your trainer

**H**ave you ever seen an ugly physical trainer? Of course not. It's so easy to fall in love with your own personal meathead, especially when he's constantly standing behind you, running his beefy hands up and down your body. And, hey, it's not a crime or unethical to hook up with a trainer. It's not like he's your gynecologist or your lawyer. But sometimes it's hard to tell if your trainer is actually after you, or if he flirts so you'll keep coming back and paying him.

## The OMG! list of signs that your trainer is using you

→ **OPTION #1: He doesn't get a boner**

If you're sticking out your chest and shaking your booty and grunting and there's absolutely no movement in his shorts, that could be a problem.

→ **OPTION #2: He actually cares about your workout**

If he's training you so hard that you look like a wet poodle by the time your session is over, chances are he's not attracted to you.

→ **OPTION #3: He's gay**

Does he dress in cuter workout clothes than you? And smell better than you after exercising? And does he keep talking about his friend Juan? Yeah, then he's just not that into you—and never will be.

## OMGesus!

Studies show that fresh male sweat attracts women—but men can boost their erections with the smell of cinnamon buns, according to a report by the Smell and Taste Research Foundation.

### THE DIFFERENCE BETWEEN A PERSONAL TRAINER AND A GIGOLO

| PERSONAL TRAINER | GIGOLO |
|---|---|
| Is paid to tell you "You look hot" | Is paid to tell you "You look hot" |
| Takes steroids | Takes Viagra |
| He will push you hard | He will bang you hard |
| Makes you do deep knee bends | Bends you over |

## >> 26. A dork is hogging the TV

**S**o you step up on the treadmill and realize you forgot your iPod. You hate running without some sort of noise to get you motivated. There's a TV overhead but some hairy, profusely sweating middle-aged man is watching, gasp, C-SPAN. How can you get pumped up, watching the Gentlemen from Wisconsin and Rhode Island debate about renewable fuels?

## The OMG! solution to dealing with a boob-tube takeover

→ **OPTION #1: Yawn loudly and often**

Yawning is contagious. Soon he will yawn and fall asleep and you can take over the remote.

→ **OPTION #2: Pretend to get hurt**

Fake faint and fall off the treadmill, like a contestant from Week 1 on *The Biggest Loser*. When he rushes to your side, tearfully ask him to go get you ice. While

he's gone, change the channel to something entertaining, such as an encore presentation of *Mother, May I Sleep with Danger?* on Lifetime starring Tori Spelling.

→ **OPTION #3: Talk back to the screen**

Act like you know a lot about politics and say, "That's right, sister!" any time House speaker Nancy Pelosi speaks. Launch into a monologue about how different the world would be today if Hillary Clinton beat Barack Obama in the primary. He'll be so annoyed, he'll get off the machine early.

## OMGesus!

TV watching burns less energy compared to other sedentary activities like sewing, reading, writing, and driving a car.

> *"When I'm on the treadmill I like either really girly music or '80s rock."*
>
> —LAUREN CONRAD

### Please Don't Stop the Music!

According to the *Journal of Exercise Physiology*, exercising to fast music—as opposed to slow or no music—burns 40 extra calories per hour.

### STARS' STRANGE FAVORITE WORKOUT TUNES

| | |
|---|---|
| Rihanna | Listens to her own music |
| Jennifer Aniston | Stevie Wonder |
| Reese Witherspoon | John Mayer and the Pussycat Dolls |
| Eva Longoria | Air Supply |
| Elizabeth Hasselbeck | Rascal Flatts |

## 27. A guy in your spin class is a grunter

You sign up for an advanced spin class, where the teacher is a ball-buster, expecting to work your tushy off. But after you hop on a stationary bike, and the music starts up, the guy next to you starts making the loudest, most annoying grunts and moans ever. Obviously, the hard seat is turning him on (or maybe his balls are being crushed, who knows?), and you actually feel like you are listening to him have sex! Every time you go to this session, you can't concentrate because he's always there groaning like a porn star. It's so distracting you might have to quit and take belly-dancing classes.

## The OMG! solution to dealing with a gym grunter

### → OPTION #1: Mock him

They say imitation is the sincerest form of flattery. Not this time. Make fun of the dude by getting off your bike, walking up to him and shrieking right in his face. Like Jamie Lee Curtis in *Halloween* screaming.

### → OPTION #2: Record him

Bring a tape recorder and capture his ridiculous cacophony of noises. After the class, follow him around wherever he goes, like the grocery store or his church, and play back the tape. He'll be stunned into silence.

## → OPTION #3: Start a petition

If complaining to the management doesn't help, draft a document stating that nobody likes the grunter or the foul sounds that come out of his mouth. Stand in front of the gym and collect 10,000 signatures.

## → OPTION #4: Have him hauled away for observation

Right before the class starts, call 911 and say that someone is passing a kidney stone in spin class. Just minutes after he starts grunting, the medics will burst into the room and take him to the hospital.

### Gym Class Hero

In 2007, in a New York City Equinox, Christopher Carter got really annoyed with Stuart Sugarman's loud exclamations—which included "You go, girl!" and "Good burn!"—during a spin class. So he picked up Sugarman's bike and threw it into a wall (with Sugarman still on it). Sugarman filed a criminal complaint but Carter was found not guilty of assault.

## OMGjesus!

Genital discomfort affects 60 percent of women cyclists. According to a study at the University of Cologne in Germany, riding a bike with your body at a 30-degree angle or less can cause a 70 percent reduction in the blood supply to the genitals. So sit up straight or suffer the consequences!

## 28. A hot guy is making a beeline for you—but you smell

**Y**ou've had a crush on this Taylor Lautner-look alike for weeks. You've made eye contact across the weight room and you catch him sneaking peeks at you in the mirror. Unfortunately, the day that he decides to finally come get your digits, you've neglected to shower and you've just taken a brutal boot camp class. You're as soaked as Whitney Houston—and flies are practically buzzing around your head.

### The OMG! solution to seducing your crush after an intense workout

#### → STEP #1: Take off your shirt

You don't want him to see you with giant sweat stains in your armpits. Remove your top and stand there in your sports bra. You know a lot of other women do that normally, so why can't you?

#### → STEP #2: Wipe your body down

Wring the sweat from your hair and rub it all over your body. You'll look like a glistening body-builder.

#### → STEP #3: Put your hair up

Get those wet hairs sticking to your face and neck up and off your face, stat.

### → STEP #4: Touch his nipple

When he walks up, lightly touch his chest and subtly brush his nipple. He'll be so turned on, he won't even notice your stench.

### → STEP #5: Ask him for a dip

Tell him you're going swimming and you'd love it if he'd join. Jump in the pool and get the odor off your body.

> *"I really don't think I need buns of steel. I'd be happy with buns of cinnamon."*
>
> —ELLEN DEGENERES

## In the Future...

In order not to stink so bad at the gym:

- Change your shoes. Don't wear the same pair two days in a row.

- Shave your underarms and use deodorant before you leave the house.

- Don't eat garlic or drink booze the night before—they will come out of your pores.

## >> 29. A gym bunny keeps talking on her cell phone

**M**ost of us go to the gym to get a real workout. But there are some women who only show up so they can walk around half-naked and pick up guys. And those are the chicks that always seem to be yapping away on their cell phones.

## The OMG! solution to shutting up a Chatty Cathy

### → OPTION #1: Harass her

Find out her number. Keep calling it and asking for either Rusty Bedsprings or saying, "Have you seen Mike Hunt?"

### → OPTION #2: Scare her

Ring her up and say, "Have you checked the children?" Or pretend to be her boyfriend's other girlfriend and ask why he's got her number programmed into his phone.

### → OPTION #3: Interrupt her

Listen in on the conversation and give your opinion on every topic she brings up.

### → OPTION #4: Stop her

Smash her phone to pieces with a ten-pound dumbbell.

> "I don't exercise. If God had wanted me to bend over, he would have put diamonds on the floor."
>
> —JOAN RIVERS

## Cell Phone Etiquette

- 61 percent of Americans believe a law banning cell phone use in public settings such as movies, restaurants, and museums would be effective, according to a study by Public Agenda.
- 50 percent of Americans have witnessed rude cell phone behavior—but only 17 percent admit that they've made inappropriate calls. . . .
- 33 percent of Americans believe it's okay to take a call in a restaurant.
- 10 percent think it's okay to pick up on a first date.

### OMGesus!

British researcher and neurosurgeon Dr. Vini Khurana believes cell phone use could kill more people than smoking! And a study in the *American Journal of Epidemiology* found that using handsets for ten years or more can double the risk of brain cancer.

You go the gym four times a week religiously. You take all the classes, including ominous-sounding ones like Step Kill. You even got a trainer for awhile. But a year and $800 later, you still look like a lard in a bikini. What gives?

## The OMG! solution for losing weight

### → OPTION #1: Stop drinking

Listen, you lush. As long as you go out partying every night, you're not going to stay skinny. Drinking five rum-and-Cokes per night packs on about 1,600 to 1,800 calories. You might as well stay home and eat six cupcakes.

### → OPTION #2: Stop rewarding yourself

Yes, you feel great after a particularly hard workout. So then don't congratulate yourself by eating an In-N-Out burger and fries animal-style afterwards!

### → OPTION #3: Eat breakfast

Get your butt out of bed and start your day earlier, you lazy bum! People who don't eat breakfast gain more weight.

## → OPTION #4: Stop pounding diet soda

According to studies, the more diet pop you drink the more weight you gain, especially in the form of lovely belly fat.

## → OPTION #5: Don't be a couch potato

People who eat fast food twice a week and spend at least two and a half hours a day watching television have triple the risk of obesity.

## → OPTION #6: Stop abusing your credit cards

Studies by major credit card companies have shown that people order more food when they plunk down the plastic instead of paying with cold hard cash.

> "Never eat more than you can lift."
>
> —MISS PIGGY

### OMGesus!

Obesity is contagious, like cooties! According to a study in the *New England Journal of Medicine*, people are more likely to become obese if their friend does! If your friend is a lard, you have a 57 percent chance of being a lard, too.

## → OPTION #7: Break up

A lot of people get really skinny when someone dumps them because they are too depressed to eat.

## → OPTION #8: Get sick

Catch swine flu and shed ten pounds in a week! It'll be worth it for the weight loss.

# chapter 4

# Relationship Killers

# 31. Your boyfriend wants you to get a boob job

**S**omehow you made it through middle school, despite constant taunts from zitty preteens calling you "tiny tits," "mosquito bites," and "brick wall." It took hard work, and some time and soul-searching, but you learned to love your body. And then, you met a nice guy who claimed he loved your little breasts, loved you just the way you are. But after dating for a year—and after catching the Hooters International Swimsuit competition on ESPN2—he suddenly asks you if you'd ever consider getting implants, and offers to pay for it. What a boob!

## The OMG! solution to avoiding plastic surgery

### → OPTION #1: Go big or go home

Tell your boyfriend you will get implants but you're going for the world record if you do. Show him a picture of Sheyla Hershey, the current record holder, who put a gallon of silicone into her 38KKK implants. Although they are in danger of exploding, Sheyla says,

"To me, big is beautiful. I don't think I have anything to worry about."

*Things you'll never hear a woman say: 'My, what an attractive scrotum!'*

—PATRICIA ARQUETTE

## →OPTION #2: Show him statistics

According to studies, women with breast implants get further ahead in the workforce. Which means you will make more money than your boyfriend, who will ultimately resent you and feel emasculated.

## →OPTION #3: Make him go to www.awfulplasticsurgery.com

When he sees the lopsided boob jobs and ugly scars from botched surgeries, he just may change his mind.

## →OPTION #4: Suggest he get pec implants

Tell your boyfriend you want him to look like Gerard Butler in *300* and that the American Society of Plastic Surgeons reports that there's been a 99 percent increase in boob jobs for men. If you can do it, so can he! You can do it together! And it only costs about $7,000!

### OMGesus!

According to the American Society for Aesthetic Plastic Surgery, most women want C cups—and they prefer round boobs over teardrop-shaped boobs.

**Famous Mangled Melons**

### Pamela Anderson

*The* Baywatch *babe has had surgery four times to make them bigger and smaller, prompting one plastic surgeon to tell the* Insider *that they are in danger of caving in.*

### Tara Reid

*The* American Pie *star's botched augmentation humiliated her and gave her, in her own words, "the ugliest boob job in the world. If I had to do it again, I would have never done it in the first place."*

### Dr. Donda West

*Kanye West's mom died on the operating table after reportedly having complications during a tummy tuck and breast augmentation.*

# 32. Your boyfriend has a wandering eye

**W**hen it comes to your snuggle bunny, you have tunnel vision—you only have eyes for him. But your significant other is always checking out other girls in front of you. You could be at a restaurant, talking in depth about the genocide in Rwanda, when suddenly his eyes move toward a beauty at the bar, then up, then down. It's not only rude, it's ego-crushing!

## The OMG! solution to obstructing ogling

### → OPTION #1: Get a dog neck cone

Make your boyfriend wear the giant collar, so he has no peripheral vision. He also will not be able to lick his own butt, which could come in handy, too.

### → OPTION #2: Squirt him with water

Every time your boyfriend checks out another chick, take a spray bottle out of your purse and shoot him right in the eye. Like Pavlov's dogs, soon he will be conditioned properly and will never take his eyes off you again.

### → OPTION #3: Check out other guys

Every time he strains his neck, take your own little look-see around the bar or restaurant and whistle when you see a hot guy. No doubt your boyfriend will not appreciate it.

## →OPTION #4: Have him genetically tested

Swedish researchers say two out of five men have a gene called an allele that makes them more likely to cheat, get divorced, and just generally be more of an asshole. If he's got this, dump him NOW.

*In the Future...*

If your man is going out with his buddies, call him right before he walks out the door. A study at Florida State University says that guys who have just been triggered to think about their relationships will be less interested in checking out other women, at least for awhile.

### OMGesus!

75 percent of married men, or men in committed relationships, cheat.

### Laws of Attraction

- Women are more attracted to men in expensive cars than in a car like a Ford Focus, English researchers have proven.
- Men are more attracted to their female subordinates than to their bosses or equal-rank coworkers, according to a study in *Evolution and Human Behavior*.
- Hungry men are more attracted to heavier women, according to the *British Journal of Psychology*. So the fatties out there should pick up guys at happy hour, before they've eaten!
- Men are attracted to women who look like their moms, Hungarian scientists say.

## 33. Your boyfriend has been posting pictures of his penis online

**S**o, you're fantasizing about the day you and your boyfriend move in together, and decide to troll around on Craigslist. com looking for your dream home. When you're on the site, the personals section catches your eye. You've always heard that the "Random Encounters" are raunchy, so what the heck, you click on "Men Seeking Women." Unbelievably, the first image to assault your eyes is a photo of your dearly beloved's member. You'd recognize that trousersnake anywhere.

### The OMG! solution to finding out your boyfriend is an exhibitionist

→ **STEP #1:** Create a fake e-mail account with a filthy name, like hotboxxx69@gmail.com.

→ **STEP #2:** Send your boyfriend an e-mail pretending to be a sexy girl named Candy Stryper. Tell him you want to meet up at a coffeehouse.

**→ STEP #3:** Meet him at the coffeehouse.

**→ STEP #4:** Hold up a picture of his penis for the entire coffeehouse to see, then pass out copies to all of the customers.

**→ STEP #5:** Make a dignified exit.

## OMGesus!

According to a CosmoGirl.com survey, 33 percent of young guys ages twenty to twenty-six and 18 percent of teen boys have posted naked pictures or videos of themselves online.

## Craigslist is More Dangerous than Detroit!

- **It's a candy store for murderers**
  Alleged Craigslist Killer Phillip Markoff allegedly used the site to meet up with at least two female massage therapists, then allegedly killed them.

- **It's easy to get robbed**
  Some fiends in Ohio posted an ad to sell an SUV. When an unsuspecting couple showed up to check the car out, they were held up at gunpoint and forced to hand over $7,000 cash.

- **It's perfect for con artists**
  Sherry Johnson Huwitt looked out her window one day and saw a truck pull up, people get out and try to take her portable basketball hoop. Her neighbor allegedly posted an ad on her behalf to sell it but never told her and kept the money.

- **It's a pimp's dream**
  The TV show *48 Hours* logged on to the site and within thirty minutes had three pay-for-play "dates."

## 34. Your boyfriend always expects you to pay for dinner

You found the perfect man—he's adorable, attentive, and committed—but there's only one problem. He's broke. So any time you want to do anything, like grab a burger, he disappears into the bathroom or you find yourself fishing in your purse for your wallet while he stares off into space. You're all for being an independent woman, but this is ridiculous!

### The OMG! solution to dealing with a cheapskate

→ **OPTION #1: Ask for a separate check**

When you go out for dinner, tell the waitress you want to only pay for yourself. Then order a lobster.

→ **OPTION #2: Don't pay**

Pull the manager aside and tell him that you are paying for yourself but not your companion and that you want to teach him a lesson. When the meal's over, get up and leave, while the manager makes your boyfriend do the dishes to pay his way.

→ **OPTION #3: Dump his tightwad ass!**

Dear Abby says a mooching boyfriend will never change. Picture a future with this loser, who will probably be on unemployment and take you out for dinner at a bar with happy hour because there are free hot dogs.

## OMGesus!

According to a survey by Jeanne Fleming and Leonard Schwarz, the authors of the book *Isn't It Their Turn to Pick Up the Check?*, 95 percent of Americans have lent money to a friend or family member—and 27 percent never got paid back! P.S.: Women are more likely to get stiffed than men.

## How to Spot a Mooch

- He steals toilet paper from public places.
- He checks out books from the library.
- He cuts his own hair like Josh Hartnett.
- He's a bad tipper.
- He never buys a round.
- He takes condiments from fast food restaurants.
- He buys Christmas presents for next year during the January discounts.
- He always says, "The next one's on me."

## Famous Freeloaders in History

Kevin Federline

Queen Elizabeth

Spencer and Heidi

Howard K. Stern

Nick Cannon

The Octomom

Kato Kaelin

Todd Palin

Oprah's boyfriend

*In the Future...*

Date a rich guy. A study at Newcastle University found that women's orgasm frequency increases with the income of her partner.

## 35. Your boyfriend might be gay

**A**dam Lambert is flaming and the Cougars love him. Boy-bander Lance Bass likes boys. Neil Patrick Harris is queer, too. In this day and age, being a homo is no big deal—unless the friend of Dorothy happens to be your boyfriend (or you live in a small town in a Red State. But that's a discussion for another day). Now you may have noticed that your significant other blow-dries his hair or wears spray tan. This does not necessarily mean he has switched teams. However, you need to ask him if he is gay, and it must be done delicately. Because many straight guys don't take too kindly to being asked if they like penis.

## The OMG! questionnaire for your potentially gay boyfriend

If your boyfriend answers "yes" to at least five of these questions, he probably is fagulous.

➔ **QUESTION #1:** Isn't Jake Gyllenhaal dreamy?

➔ **QUESTION #2:** Hugh Jackman is so much better on Broadway than in those awful Wolverine movies, isn't he?

➔ **QUESTION #3:** Is it just my imagination, or are Zac Efron's eyes really as blue as the summer sky?

→ **QUESTION #4:** Don't you think Miss California is a dumb bitch?

→ **QUESTION #5:** Should Ryan Seacrest keep frosting his hair?

### OMGesus!

The Kinsey Reports say that 37 percent of men have had a homosexual experience (and no, that doesn't include watching *The Notebook*).

## QUIZ: HOMO SAY WHAT?

Match the celebrity with their denial that they are gay.

1. Hugh Jackman
2. Jared Leto
3. Kenny Chesney
4. Ed Westwick and Chase Crawford
5. John Mayer

A. By denying it, I'm saying there's something shameful about it.
B. I'm gay . . . as a goose.
C. It's not true. Period.
D. We are so into women it's ridiculous.
E. You're damn right I made out with Perez Hilton.

*1-A, 2-B, 3-C, 4-D, 5-E

## SIGNS OF SEXUAL ORIENTATION

| STRAIGHT | METROSEXUAL | DRAG QUEEN |
|---|---|---|
| Has bedhead | Has highlights | Has extensions |
| Wallet in back pocket | Carries a man purse | Carries a woman's purse |
| Smelly balls | Shaves balls | Tapes balls |
| Waxes chest | Waxes eyebrows | Waxes everything |
| Bites nails | Gets manicure | Has acrylic nails |

# 36. Your boyfriend is an obnoxious drunk

Your beau is sweet as pie when he's sober. But as soon as he has a case of beer and a couple of shots of Jack Daniels, he turns into a monster. He's belligerent, gets in fights, cries like a girl, and frequently gets naked in public places. The next day, you have to apologize to a half-dozen people, and often have to pay to repair something, like a broken window.

## The OMG! solution to dealing with a boozehound

### → OPTION #1: Point out his beer belly

Men are vain, too, and don't like to be told they're fat. Rub his belly and give it its own name, like Marvin. He won't think it's funny and will embark on a fitness regimen that will not include alcohol.

### → OPTION #2: Contact *Intervention*

Call the TV show producers and give them your boyfriend's name.

They will film him being a drunk then offer him rehab. He will say yes and go away for three months and come back a changed man. But then he'll be a local celebrity for being on *Intervention* and the pressures of fame will turn him back to the bottle. So never mind. Don't call *Intervention*.

### → OPTION #3: Act like a rat

Call the cops on him when he's drunk. A night in the slammer, with a giant crackhead named Tiny, will scare him straight.

### → OPTION #4: Be worse

If you can't beat him, join him. The only way to make sure he's not out of control is to be out of control yourself. Drink until you puke. He'll have no choice but to take care of you and hold your hair back.

*In the Future...*

Activities to try instead of drinking:

- Knitting
- Stamp collecting
- Writing computer programs
- Going to church
- Conducting alien autopsies
- Solving jigsaw puzzles

## OMGesus!

41 percent of college students are binge drinkers, meaning they drink four or more drinks in a night out. And studies show that women bingers have more unprotected sex, anal sex, and higher rates of gonorrhea, bladder explosions, and depression! Sounds awesome!

**Sexy Guys with Beer Bellies**

Tony Soprano

Jack Black

Seth Rogen

Kevin Federline

Hurley on *Lost*

*FYI*

American men account for 75 percent of beer drinking, compared to just 25 percent for American women, says DrinkFocus.com.

## 37. Your boyfriend's friends are jerks

**Y**our boyfriend's buddies are mean to you and you have no idea why. You've met them a thousand times and they either ignore you, make fun of you to your face, or exclude you from inside jokes they've all had since they were six years old. Your man insists that nothing's wrong but you can tell they despise you. But you'll stop at nothing to win them over.

## The OMG! solution to getting on the good side of his pussy posse

### → OPTION #1: Cook for them

They way to a man's heart is through his stomach. Throw a dinner party and serve up a manly menu, like burgers, ribs, wings, and nachos. They'll warm up to you in no time.

### → OPTION #2: Bring hot girls around

Instead of showing up by yourself, drag along your sexiest pals. The guys will be so busy flirting, they won't have time to hate your every fiber.

### → OPTION #3: Let him watch sports

Be the cool girl and allow him to have ESPN on all the time when his buddies are over.

### → OPTION #4: Don't tag along

Guys hate it when girlfriends show up unexpectedly to their nights out. Let him be free and go in peace.

### → OPTION #5: Don't emasculate him

Stop calling him pet names like Pookie, Snuggle Bear, or Schnookums in front of his pals.

## OMGesus!

A decade-long study at the University of Michigan about male bonding shows that adult male chimps usually have seven-year friendships with other males, and like to exchange back scratches, share meat, and chum around.

## How to Tell If Your Friends Hate Your Boyfriend

- They never ask you about him.
- They try to set you up with other guys.
- They roll their eyes when you talk about him.
- They give you self-help books.
- They always cancel plans with both of you.
- They have mean nicknames for him.
- They say they hate him.

# 38. He's still friends with his ex

Your boyfriend has professed his undying love for you—and only you—and yet there seems to be another person lurking about in your relationship. His annoying ex! Somehow, he's one of those guys that can remain on good terms with a former girlfriend. And while you trust him, you definitely don't trust her. You know she's still in love with him. You can tell by the flirtatious posts she leaves on his Facebook page. He claims to be oblivious, but something fishy is going on here . . . .

## The OMG! solution to getting rid of an ex-girlfriend

→ **OPTION #1: Find her a new man**

Pay your hottest but most commitment-phobic friend to take her out. He can seduce her then break her heart, giving her something else to obsess about other than your boyfriend.

→ **OPTION #2: Point out her flaws**

Mention that women usually end up looking like their mothers. Make it clear that his ex's mother is a heifer.

### → OPTION #3: Sign her up for the Peace Corps

Fill out an online application for her and make her accomplishments shine. Mark down that if she's accepted, she'd like to work in Swaziland for the next twenty-seven months.

### → OPTION #4: Befriend her

Keep your enemies close. Act like you two are BFFs. Start inviting her out with you and your boyfriend. Make out with him in front of her. When she finally sees how in love you two are, she'll finally get the hint that she needs to move on.

### → OPTION #5: Grow some balls

Tell your boyfriend he'd better stop taking her calls or you're walking out the do'!

## OMGesus!

Can't we all just get along? A Nurses' Health Study from Harvard Medical School found that the more friends women had, the less likely they were to develop physical impairments as they aged. We all want to look like hot cougars, so let's stop fighting over men!

## Ex-tremely Nasty Fights

### Jennifer Aniston vs. Angelina Jolie

*Angelina stole Jen's husband away but Jen has made sure to stick it to the femme fatale in practically every interview. She's called Angie "uncool" and revealed that she sent Brad congratulation texts after the births of his babies. Brad has also admitted that he still talks to his ex. "Jen is a sweetheart," he told W. "We still check in with each other."*

### Giselle Bundchen vs. Bridget Moynihan

*New England Patriot QB Tom Brady can never get rid of his ex, Bridget, because he had a baby with her. Giselle totally dissed her publicly when she told Vanity Fair magazine, "It's not like because somebody else delivered him, that's not my child. I love him the same way as if he were mine. I already feel like he's my son, from the first day." Meow!*

### Heather Locklear vs. Denise Richards

*Denise reportedly encouraged her former BFF to divorce her husband, Bon Jovi guitarist Richie Sambora, then started dating him. Heather was pissed off but took the high road, saying nada. Denise couldn't keep her trap shut, telling Redbook magazine, "Did I question the decision? Yes. Did I know it wouldn't go over well? Of course. I'm a grown woman and I know what I did and the repercussions of it."*

# 39. Your boyfriend has no style

**H**e's got a cute face and rock-solid abs, but your boyfriend is lacking one physical attribute—the ability to dress himself. He wears socks with sandals and owns jean shorts, and his idea of formal wear is a button-down shirt without a mustard stain on it. He needs some serious help. Luckily, men can be made over very easily. You just have to do it slowly and subtly.

## The OMG! solution to giving your man a makeover

→ **STEP #1: Hats off**

No more baseball caps. And rinse out all that gel in his hair—he looks like a guy from Jersey Shore! And that's not a compliment.

→ **STEP #2: Wax on**

Hairy backs and brows are definite turn-offs. Chest hair is optional.

→ **STEP #3: 3-2-1 contacts**

Dorothy Parker once said, "Men seldom make passes at girls who wear glasses." Well, the opposite holds true, too. The only guy in the entire universe who can really pull off geeky glasses is Clark Kent. Otherwise, spectacles are for Mr. Magoo and Sarah Palin. Of course, sunglasses make everybody look good, as long as they're not those cheesetastic Oakleys.

→ **STEP #4: Brief him**

Tighty-whities are underpants for little boys. Men look best in boxer briefs. Oh, here's a funny joke:

Why does Bill Clinton wear boxers? To keep his ankles warm!

### →STEP #5: Pull his pants up

Dude, it's not okay for your boyfriend's ass to be hanging over his pants. It's going to be hard to ask him to raise 'em up, but butter him up. Say how sexy his butt is and you can't tell when his pants hang so low. Also, tell him that Barack Obama wants him to. "Brothers should pull up their pants!" the Prez told MTV. "You are walking by your mother, your grandmother, your underwear is showing. What's wrong with that? Come on. Some people might not want to see your underwear—I'm one of them."

And when he says "Brothers," he means black and white bros.

*In the Future...*

Don't drag your boyfriend to the store—just pick up stuff for him. A British researcher has concluded that shopping is literally bad for a man's health and could make his blood pressure rise to dangerous levels! No wonder they always need to sit down in those chairs!

"I don't really see the point in washing your hair. I have my hair for just, you know, hanging out on my head. I don't care if it's clean or not."

—ROBERT PATTINSON

**Y**ou like to play Fallout as much as the next guy. But being abducted by aliens gets a tad boring after a couple of hours. Your boyfriend, on the other hand, can play all night—and probably will. As soon as he sits down, he starts to ignore you and his eyes glaze over like a jelly donut. You could have spiders coming out of your eyes and snakes coming out of your butt and he still wouldn't take his gaze away from the giant flatscreen overtaking his living room.

## The OMG! solution to peeling your guy's hands off his joystick

### → OPTION #1: Vacuum naked

If that doesn't get his attention, he needs serious help.

### → OPTION #2: Provide viable options

Obviously he's not going to leave the house if you tell him you have tickets to the ballet. So tempt him with something you both like,

such as a Monster Truck rally or putt-putt golf.

### → OPTION #3: Sabotage

When he finally passes out, remove the flux capacitor from the gaming widget. Those aren't real technology terms, but basically, ruin the game. If you can't figure out the wires, "accidentally" pour a glass of water on the box. But don't touch it and get electrocuted!

→ **OPTION #4: Kill your TV**

Pull an Elvis Presley and shoot a bullet right through the telly.

## OMGesus!

More Americans play video games than go to the movies. Even England's old Queen Elizabeth is a gamer. CBS News reported that she got a gold-plated Wii after becoming addicted to Prince William's Wii during the Christmas holidays.

**Is your man an addict?**

Young guys average eighteen hours of gaming per week and 8.5 percent are clinically addicted, according to a study at Iowa State University. Does your boyfriend exhibit these signs?

- He calls in sick to work when a new game comes out.
- He sneaks in playtime when everyone is sleeping.
- He doesn't eat or bathe because he can't stop.
- He can't masturbate because he has calluses and carpal tunnel.
- He has nosebleeds (oh wait, that's cocaine addiction. Never mind!).

### Barmy Brits!

72 percent of British men would rather play video games than have sex, a PlayStation3 study found.

# Chapter 5

# Dating
# Dealbreakers

# 41. He's a bad kisser

**Y**ou've had a crush on him for weeks. He finally asks you on a date and as the night goes on, you wait with anticipation for the perfect moment when he'll lean in for the kiss. You're hoping it will be sexy and passionate, like when Edward Cullen first laid lips on Bella Swan. But instead of a hot vampire kiss, you get a darting lizard tongue. Plus, he slobbers and bites too hard. What a huge letdown! Can this relationship be saved?

## The OMG! solution for sloppy smoochers

### → STEP #1: Take the lead

There's no need to crush his ego by telling him that he's the worst kisser in the history of kissing. Just take command of the situation.

### → STEP #2: Give positive and negative reinforcement

Just like those people in that shock experiment, any time his amphibian tongue appears, bite his nose—hard. But when he does something right, squeeze his arm or moan softly to show him he's on the right track.

### OMGesus!

Talk about the kiss of death! French kissing with multiple partners increases a teenager's chance of getting a fatal brain infection. Seriously. A study in the *British Medical Journal* said so.

## → STEP #3: Wipe your face on his shirt

He'll get the idea that he needs to stop drooling.

### OMGesus!

Better make it good! First impressions are lasting impressions. A study at the University of Albany showed that 59 percent of men and 66 percent of women reported that after feeling attracted to another person initially, the attraction ended after the first kiss.

## → STEP #4: Pretend to play teacher/student

Guys like that fantasy. So he's your new pupil and then you can show him step by step how to kiss. And tell him if he doesn't do what you say, you'll give him an F in kissing class.

### A Kiss Is Not Just a Kiss

- People get more excited from eating chocolate than they do when they passionately kiss their lovers.
- Kissing reduces stress.
- Women need more than a kiss to get horny. Most also need dim lighting and romantic music.
- Men are twice as likely as women to have sex with a bad kisser.

*"The first kiss I had was the most disgusting thing in my life. The girl injected about a pound of saliva into my mouth, and when I walked away I had to spit it all out."*

—LEONARDO DICAPRIO

# 42. He tells everyone you slept together (when you didn't)

**Y**ou thought you had an innocent date with a gentleman. But the next day, your cell phone is blowing up. All of your friends are hearing that you did the nasty with him—and they've got details. Locker room talk? How very classy. And so bogus! You didn't even touch the guy!

## The OMG! solution to quelling the rumors

### → STEP #1: Gather evidence

Go back to your date spot. Interview witnesses and take pictures and get copies of receipts and the security camera videotape.

### → STEP #2: Create a blog called *johnsmithisaliar.com.*

Post all evidence that shows where you were the night before and what time you got home, proving that it would be impossible to complete a sexual act.

### → STEP #3: Blast it

Send the link to all of your and John Smith's friends.

### → STEP #4: Drop out of school

With all your crack investigative work, you could probably get a job as a reporter for the *New York Times.* Or at least maybe appear on the *Today* show and be interviewed by Meredith Viera or Matt Lauer.

## OMGesus!

Men overestimate the number of sexual partners they've had, a University of Alberta study found. Another study found that women reported an average of 8.6 sexual partners and men an average of 31.9! And, of course, 21 percent of men admitted they just made up a number off the top of their heads.

### Liar or Lothario?

NBA star Wilt Chamberlain said in his 1991 biography *A View from Above,* that he bedded 20,000 women. Which would have meant that he'd have to had sex with 1.2 women every day for forty-eight years. "I'm not boasting," he wrote.

### Kiss and Tell

Women talk more about their sex lives with their friends than men do, according to a study by Penn State University. The other topics they talk about couldn't be more different. Random, but true, check out our favorite talk topics here:

- Menstruation
- STDs
- Contraception
- Rape
- Dating
- Abstinence
- Making out
- Pregnancy

Men are more likely to talk about these topics:

- Um, masturbation

## >> 43. You dumped him—but he won't go away

The date was going fine, until he mentioned that his interests include speaking Latin, playing with his collection of *Star Trek* figurines, and fiddling with his homemade time machine. At the end of the night, you tell him you just want to be friends, but this socially inept weirdo just doesn't get the hint. He bombards you with texts, e-mails, and IMs and even sends flowers to your job. Oh no, what if he's built a shrine to you in his bedroom?

## The OMG! best excuses to get rid of a harmless stalker

### → OPTION #1: You're converting

Tell the nerd that Jesus has taken the wheel, that you are giving your life over to God and becoming a nun. And that, effective immediately, you have taken a vow of celibacy and sworn off all worldly possessions, including computers and cell phones.

### → OPTION #2: You joined the CIA

Unfortunately this means you have to go undercover in Dubai. To ensure your safety, you also must change all of your e-mail and IM addresses and make them private and secure. You will no longer be able to be in contact with him.

## OMGjesus!

You can let someone else do the dirty work for you. Give your unwanted suitor the Rejection Line number (212-479-7990). When he calls, he will get a message that says, "The person who gave you this number does not want to talk to you or see you again." The dumped person can then be forwarded to a comfort specialist or hear a sad poem. For more info, check out *www.rejectiononline.com*.

### → OPTION #3: You're getting a sex change

Being around him made you realize you've always wanted to be a man. You are flying to Thailand to have an operation and would like to be known as Doug from now on.

### → OPTION #4: You're getting married

Let him know that your ex-boyfriend Vlad, who lives abroad in Uzbekistan, wants to move to America and needs you to marry him so he can live here legally and permanently.

### → OPTION #5: You died

Have a friend call him and tell him you choked on a Chewy Spree and passed away. Set up a fake funeral. Go in a disguise and see how distraught he is. If his consuming grief and wailing touches your heart, pretend it was all a big joke, yell "Surprise," and then date him. After all, nobody will ever love you like he does.

## 44. You get a period stain on your pants during a date

**Y**ou're at the movies, and all of a sudden you experience a familiar feeling. Oh yes, it's unmistakable. Your monthly bill has arrived, and, of course, you're wearing white. Unfortunately, you're not one of those OCD people, who mark down every period in a calendar. So remembering when your little friend is coming is a crapshoot.

## The OMG! solution to covering up a bloody mess

### → OPTION #1: Create a decoy

Run out to the snack bar and get a bunch of mustard and ketchup packages. Squirt them all over your pants. Go back and enjoy the movie, and when your date asks what happened, say that someone must have left the condiments on the seat and they exploded all over you. Nobody will see the period stain with all of the other crap on your clothes.

### → OPTION #2: Use the seat cushion

Just like on an airplane, the seats can be multipurpose. When your date goes to the bathroom, carve out a makeshift maxi pad from the cushion using your car keys, unbutton your pants, and stick it between your legs. It might not solve the stain problem—but at least it'll stop the floodgates!

### → OPTION #3: Call a friend

Everyone hates when people talk on their cells during a movie. So be really obnoxious on your phone, so someone complains to the manager. You will be dragged out in the dark and your date won't see the unsightly stain.

### → OPTION #4: Take your pants off

Do it subtly and throw them under the seat with your discarded popcorn tub and Junior Mint box. Then pull your shirt down and pretend it's a dress.

You get a period stain on your pants during a date **< OMG!** |

## OMGesus!

Women with PMS are total slackers! A study by Dr. Jeff Borenstein of Cedars-Sinai Medical Center in L.A. found that the raging bitches worked 14 percent fewer hours per week and got 15 percent less done in their jobs than women who are lucky enough not to get PMS (um, anyone know any women who don't get PMS??).

### On This Day in History:

**1845**—*A woman in England is acquitted for shoplifting because she is deemed temporarily insane from PMS.*

**1893**—*The lawyer for alleged ax-murderer Lizzie Borden blames her "monthly indisposition" for causing her to kill her parents.*

**1894**—*Some guys named Lombrosso and Ferrero do a study and say that of eighty women arrested for "resistance to public officials," seventy-one were menstruating.*

**1945**—*The American Journal of Obstetrics and Gynecology reports that 84 percent of all female violent crimes in Paris were done while the perps were on the rag.*

**1968**—*Some dudes named Wallach and Rubin do a study where they find that 45 percent of attempted suicides by females happened the week before menstruation.*

**1971**—*In a North Carolina prison study, 41 percent of inmate assaults happened during PMS.*

**1980**—*A barmaid named Sandie Craddock stabs a coworker to death after becoming a "raging animal" once a month.*

**1991**—*A woman is acquitted of drunk driving after her attorney argues that alcohol exacerbated her PMS!*

# 45. He's a mama's boy

You've only been on a couple of dates and you're on the fence. There's something a little off about this guy. He's always talking about how his mother is his best friend and comparing you to her. Then, the next time he picks you up for a night out, he says he has a surprise and won't tell you where you're going. You're thinking the Kenny Chesney concert—but suddenly he pulls into a driveway on a quiet cul-de-sac and a portly woman waves from the window. OMG!, he's bringing you home!

## The OMG! solution to winning over his parents

### → STEP #1: Tone it down

Using the passenger mirror, wipe off your makeup so you don't look like a French whore.

### → STEP #2: Conceal the cleavage

Bundle up the boobies as much as possible. If your date has a jacket,

you might want to consider throwing that on.

### → STEP #3: Come bearing gifts

You weren't born in a barn so you know you can't show up empty-handed. Before you go inside, sneak into the neighbor's yard and pick some fresh flowers.

### → STEP #4: Be a big phony

Even though you are livid and freaked out, greet his folks with a smile and make pleasant conversation about inane topics, such as the weather, butter cookie recipes, and the Tamil Tiger rebels in Sri Lanka.

### → STEP #5: Case the joint

Even though you so don't want to be there, take the opportunity to look around and see if he comes from money. Because if he's rich, that may make him a little more appealing. Don't lie, you know it's true . . . .

### → STEP #6: Pretend to like dinner

Even if her brisket is as dry as the Mojave and as tough as Madonna's biceps, eat it all up and compliment the chef.

### → STEP #7: Help with the dishes

Even though there are crusty dishes sitting in your own sink at home, as soon as the meal's over, be a big brownnose and get your ass up and clear the table.

## → STEP #8: Pass judgment silently

Yes, you noticed that his mother burps a lot and that his dad was ogling your bosom. But keep that to yourself and file it away in your mental Rolodex for a rainy day.

> "My mother never saw the irony in calling me a son-of-a-bitch."
>
> —JACK NICHOLSON

## Famous Mama's Boys

**Shia LaBeouf:** "Probably the sexiest woman I know is my mother. She's an ethereal angel. If I could meet my mother and marry her, I would."

**Justin Timberlake:** "I will never find someone as good as my mother. We're best friends—she's a very special woman."

**Leonardo DiCaprio:** "My mom is the only person I'd really buy [diamonds] for."

# 46. He has a kid

So you're at dinner having a fabulous time, when your f*** buddy says the seven words all women dread: "There's something I need to tell you." Turns out, your new beau is a stud—literally. Just like Levi Johnston and Bristol Palin, he accidentally got some girl pregnant and she ended up having the baby. Now, every other weekend, he plays Mr. Mom. He wants to know if you are weirded out by this—and, if not, if you'd like to meet the little rugrat and take him to Six Flags! You really don't want to, nor do you want to deal with his crazy baby mama.

## The OMG! solution to replacing the baby mama in the child's eyes

→ **STEP #1: Spoil it**

Always bring it toys and candy and let it drink soda and stay up late.

→ **STEP #2: Tickle it**

### OMGesus!

85 percent of young guys who knock a girl up do not play any active role in the kid's upbringing, according to an article in *Teen Health and Wellness*.

→ **STEP #3: Never yell at it**

→ **STEP #4: Do arts and crafts**

Kids love that shit.

→ **STEP #5: Let it wear whatever it wants**

→ **STEP #6: Give it money**

→ **STEP #7: Disparage the baby mama**

*In the Future...*

Think of this as a business opportunity. If the child is even remotely attractive, start volunteering to baby-sit. Secretly take it on auditions for commercials and catalogues. If it works out, you can be its manager and embezzle all of its money because it's a kid and it will know nothing about finances. Then you can disappear to Tahiti with the earnings and retire.

# 47. He's really religious—and you're a heathen

**W**hen you start to get to know a guy, certain topics are off limits so you don't end up hating each other. These topics include exes, abortion, sexual habits, your political affiliation, and, of course, religion. But that's dumb. Why hold off knowing the cold-hard truth about someone? You'll waste less time if you cut to the chase. Like, maybe you wouldn't have gone on three dates with this guy if you knew he was a born-again virgin, who witnesses on the beach and holds bible study class at his place every Wednesday night.

## The OMG! solution to dating a Bible thumper

→ **OPTION #1: Make him a sinner**

Using your wily ways, you could try to corrupt and seduce him. But then you'll burn in hell for eternity. And that doesn't sound like much fun.

→ **OPTION #2: Convert**

Maybe it's time for a big change in your life. You've been aimless for so long and you have really bad karma left over from all that backstabbing you did in high school. Go into the light. Seek answers. It's time for some spiritual enlightenment.

### → OPTION #3: Join a new religion together

If you really like each other, but you can't bring yourself to convert to his team, you could always join a new sect together. Trendy options these days include Scientology, in which you could be lucky enough to have Tom Cruise brainwash you; Wicca, a combination of religion and magic; and Buddhism, which just means all you really need to do is read that Oprah Book Club selection *Eat Pray Love*. It's good.

> OMGesus!
>
> New research from Harvard University found that 30 to 40 percent of young Americans say they have no religious affiliation at all.

> "Maybe there is no actual place called hell. Maybe hell is just having to listen to our grandparents breathe through their noses when they're eating sandwiches."
>
> —JIM CARREY

### → OPTION #4: Create a new faith

The Mormons did it a couple hundred years ago. So did David Koresh and those other cult people who wore the Nikes and killed themselves in those bunk beds. All you need is a little charisma, a mission statement, and some very gullible friends to follow you.

### → OPTION #5: There aren't any more. Those are pretty much the only ones.

# 48. He smokes like a chimney

**W**hen you first started going out, he was on his best behavior. He didn't get stoopid drunk, he called when he said he would, and he hid his nastiest habit—smoking cigarettes. But now, he's gotten a little too comfortable around you, and the truth is, he's got like a pack-a-day addiction. So now when you kiss him, he tastes like an ashtray. His clothes stink, and when he wakes up in the morning he coughs up a lung or two. This is not what you signed up for!

## The OMG! solution to helping him kick the butts

### → OPTION #1: Condition him

Pavlov's dogs were trained to salivate every time a bell rang. You can do something similar. Every time your boyfriend inhales, punch him in the nuts. Eventually he will associate smoking with a pain that feels like getting hit in the stomach with a giant hammer.

### → OPTION #2: Quit drinking

Studies show that a big hindrance to stopping is binge drinking. So you can both go dry until he figures it out . . . yeah right. Like you're both gonna quit drinking. Besides, only 11 percent of binge drinkers successfully stop smoking. Moving on . . . .

### → OPTION #3: Scare him

Some smokers have to have their limbs amputated because smoking cuts off oxygen to your feet and hands. Find pictures on the Internet and tape them to his pack of smokes.

### → OPTION #4: Replace the addiction

When alcoholics get sober, they often replace the addiction of drinking with going to twelve-step meetings obsessively. Your guy needs something to replace his oral fixation, so he should probably go down on you twenty times a day.

### → OPTION #5: Find him new friends

Smokers are like gang members. Once you quit, you are excommunicated from the group. Ex-smokers often find after quitting that they really had nothing in common with their smoking buddies anyway, other than putting cancer sticks in their mouths.

## OMGesus!

In New York City, smokers spend an average of $2,500 per year on packs of cigarettes, according to a poll conducted by the city's Department of Health and Mental Hygiene in 2007.

### Poor Patrick Wasn't Sway-zied by Statistics

The *Dirty Dancing* star may have been dying from pancreatic cancer, but Patrick, who had a three-pack-a-day habit, was still spotted chain-smoking outside the treatment center where he got chemo. When asked by Barbara Walters why he hadn't quit, the tough old boot replied, "It's not my priority." RIP, Patrick. We love you, man.

## 49. He's obsessed with sex

You barely know the guy but he feels strangely comfortable talking about sex all the time in front of you. You could be discussing the Palestinian-Israeli conflict and he will find a way to tell you that Golda Meir makes his soldier stand at attention. When you IM, he tries to get you to type dirty to him. And if you're out together, he spots hot girls and asks if you'd do a threesome with him. Here's the problem: If he was ugly, it'd totally be sexual harassment! But he's cute, so it kind of turns you on. But you're not ready and he's pressuring you! But you also don't want to lose him . . . .

## The OMG! excuses for stalling a horny toad

### →OPTION #1: Duh, your period

Of course, that will only work once for one week. So use that card wisely.

### →OPTION #2: You forgot to take the pill

Your cycle is all off and you don't want to get pregnant.

## →OPTION #3: Razor burn

Tell him you shaved it all off down there and you used a dull razor and now you're too sensitive and itchy.

### OMGjesus!

30 percent of women who use online dating services have had sex on the first date, according to Sexuality Research & Social Policy. But that's not a good idea. Another study from University College London found that avoiding sex with a partner on the first date is key to making it work long-term.

## →OPTION #4: You're ill

Cough and pretend like you have a cold and a fever.

## →OPTION #5: Your friend needs you

Say that your BFF just got dumped and needs you tonight.

## →OPTION #6: Start a fight

It can be about anything. That way, you can storm off and avoid having sex, yet still have sexual tension!

### Dirty Dogs!

According to an ABC *Primetime Live* poll:

- 70 percent of men think about sex every day (only 34 percent of women do)
- 57 percent of Americans have had sex outdoors
- 51 percent of women like to have sex with the lights off
- 50 percent of women have faked orgasms
- 31 percent of men sleep in the nude
- 15 percent of men have paid for sex

## 50. He's short

This guy is crazy about you. He's attractive, he has a good job, he makes decent money, and he's funny too. But there's a "big" problem—he's like 5'5". Unfortunately, he doesn't have a Napoleon complex so instead of overcompensating with a huge personality, he's very shy and sensitive about his height. And to be honest, you feel awkward standing next to him and bending down to kiss him. Plus his hands and feet are smaller than yours—not a good sign.

## The OMG! solution to dating a little person

### → STEP #1: Wear flats at all times

Nicole Kidman did that when she was married to Tom Cruise, who is notoriously short. But after they divorced, she made fun of him, saying, "Now I can wear heels."

### → STEP #2: Buy him lifts

Supposedly, Tom Cruise wears these. And if you notice, his shoes always have a little bit of a heel, too.

### OMGesus!

In the U.S., the average man is 5'9", says a National Health and Nutrition Examination Survey. But Japanese males are, on average, at least 10 centimeters shorter than Western dudes, an article by the Sumitomo Group Public Affairs Committee claims.

### → STEP #3: Hunch your shoulders

Sure, you could get a hump on your back, but it'll be worth it if this is the man you plan to marry and have a family with.

### → STEP #4: Sit down in pictures

That way he won't look like a midget in all of your photos.

### → STEP #5: Practice dancing in private

Get a system down so that when you're in public, you don't look like his mother chaperoning a school dance.

### → STEP #6: Don't pick him up or muss his hair

Ever.

**Short and Sssss-weet Men**

Jon Stewart

Bono

Picasso

Stalin

Mini-Me

David Archuleta

Kurt Cobain

Ja Rule

King Tut

Curly from the Three Stooges

Gandhi

---

### BENEFITS AND RISKS OF DATING AN ELF

| Benefits | Risks |
| --- | --- |
| Are less likely to lose their temper | Are more likely to be pedophiles |
| Are popular | Are more likely to be jealous |
| Are more likely to stay childless (could also be a risk) | Earn less money |

OMG!

# Chapter 6

# Eat, Pray, Shop

# 51. A cheapskate always wants to split the bill

**Y**ou know the guy. A group goes out for dinner and, while you nibble on a simple salad and a Diet Coke, he orders several top-shelf cocktails, an appetizer, the most expensive entree, and dessert. And, of course, when the bill comes, he thinks you should all split it evenly! So you end up paying for most of his dinner . . . again.

## The OMG! solution to making people pay their fair share

### → OPTION #1: Make him be the collector

The person who actually holds the bill always gets screwed. Nobody ever puts in enough, and when you're short, the person holding the bill always ends up digging back in his or her wallet for more cash.

### → OPTION #2: Eat his food

Since you're paying for his lobster, reach over to his plate, snap off a claw and dip it in the butter dish.

If he looks at you incredulously, say, "Since I bought this, I want my fair share." While you're at it, wash it down with his Ketel One martini.

> ### OMGesus!
>
> According to an Associated Press article, in 2007, a Pizza Hut waitress in Indiana received a $10,000 tip from a regular customer who found out she couldn't afford college!

## → OPTION #3: Itemize

People hesitate to do this because it makes YOU look like a cheap-wad, but if there is a huge discrepancy in what people ate and drank you should have no shame saying that you are only paying for what you ordered. The rules have changed since the recession.

### Can't We All Just Get Along?

We all know that waiters and customers have a strained relationship. Here are some of customers' biggest complaints about waiters and vice versa:

**Customers about Waiters**

- They tack on a gratuity without telling you.
- They sneak extra filet mignons onto the bill.
- They don't write down the order. Don't do that! You always get it wrong!
- They knock into you every time they walk by.
- They don't know what the soup of the day is.

**Waiters about Customers**

- They're too lazy to do the math and just double the tax for the tip. In some states, that doesn't even come to 15 percent.
- They send back food.
- They stay too long at the table during peak hours.
- They have the Harry Met Sally syndrome: adding and taking a million things off the order and faking orgasms at the table.
- They have filthy kids.
- They tip with change.
- They tell me their life story.

## >> 52. Birthday dinners are bankrupting you

**N**ow that you have 600 friends on Facebook, you're quite popular and your calendar is full. But the downside of this is that practically every day, you get another invite to a birthday party. And while you feel obligated to show up to most of these events, you also feel obligated to bring some sort of gift, like wine or a generic candle. Also, these giant birthday dinners, with twenty or more people, get really expensive! Everybody orders booze with abandon and you have to pay for the guest of honor, so you always end up forking out like $100! You're going to have to pick and choose your birthday dinners more wisely—without offending the other birthday boys' and girls' feelings.

## The OMG! solution to choosing which birthday parties to go to

### → OPTION #1: Special occasions only

Milestone birthdays, like twenty-one or thirty, are no-brainers. But don't feel required to celebrate someone's, like, twenty-third birthday. What's the big deal?

### → OPTION #2: Cheap eats

When the menu is limited to basic stuff like pizza or burgers, you're pretty safe. But when the parties are held at trendy restaurants, that's when the bill goes apeshit.

### → OPTION #3: They're rich

People with extremely affluent parents may just plop down their plastic at the end of the meal. But this is risky and shouldn't be counted on.

### → OPTION #4: It's a hotspot

If this party is at a place that's impossible to get into, you should go because it may be your only shot at hanging out with the pretty people.

### → OPTION #5: It's got a good guest list

See who else is going. If you think you'll be sandwiched between the girl who only talks about her boring job and the guy who smells like Polish sausage, skip it.

### → OPTION #6: Chef's tasting

Don't do it. It costs a fortune and you only end up getting like a piece of lettuce and a meatball.

## OMGesus!

Researchers at the University of Missouri have wasted money on a study, published in the *Journal of Consulting and Clinical Psychology*, that proves that twenty-one-year-olds often try to do twenty-one shots on their birthdays, putting their health at risk. Um, duh! In fact, 34 percent of men and 24 percent of women admit that they had twenty-one drinks to celebrate that momentous occasion! The maximum for men was fifty drinks, thirty for women. Okay, now that's a bit excessive . . . .

### Birthday Blowouts

- Suri Cruise's second birthday bash reportedly cost $100,000 and included a $5,000 cake.
- The Sultan of Brunei's fiftieth birthday soiree cost $27 million and included a private concert by Michael Jackson.
- Jay-Z bought Beyoncé a $1 million Rolls Royce for her twenty-fifth birthday.

# >> 53. Your credit card is maxed out

You've waited in line for like five hours at Old Navy because even though there are a million customers, they only have two employees at the registers. So everyone is already pissed off and edgy. You finally make it to the front of the queue and the cashier rings up your cute new tops and skirts. But when he runs your plastic through the machine—DECLINED. You don't have any cash and that's your only credit card. Yeah, this is pretty mortifying. And everybody's watching! After laughing uproariously, tell the cashier that your business manager must have put your monthly inheritance stipend in the wrong account, pretend to make a call to said business manager, and slink out the door.

## The OMG! solution to getting out of debt so you're never humiliated again

### → OPTION #1: Sell your eggs

You can earn up to $7,000 for just one donation from your woman-parts. The downside is that you have to be twenty-one, you can only give them away six times, and you may experience hot flashes, headaches, and vision problems.

### → OPTION #2: Smuggle in exotic animals

Importing birds, snakes, monkeys, and other wildlife into the U.S. from Latin America is a $10 billion a year industry, second only to drug smuggling! So you could make serious cash, as long as you don't catch animal diseases like tularemia or lymphocytic choriomeningitis and die.

### → OPTION #3: Play for the New York Yankees

The MLB team spent $201 million on salaries in 2009, including $33 million to A-Rod and $1.2 million to some guy named Brian Bruney, according to figures compiled by the Associated Press and the Major League Baseball Players Association. Exactly. If Brian Bruney can make $1.2 million, why can't you? Time to hit the batting cage!

### → OPTION #4: Become a pimp

Surely you have some sexy friends who also want to make some serious dough? Rent the movie *Risky Business*—which stars a young, handsome, not-crazy Tom Cruise—to learn how to start your own brothel.

## OMGesus!

The average credit card balance for graduating college seniors is about $4,100, according to a 2009 report by Sallie Mae. That's a lotsa mozzarella!

### → OPTION #5: Murder for hire

It's simple. Place an ad in *Soldier of Fortune* (or on Craigslist, see Chapter 3, #33). Buy a gun from Wal-Mart. Kill someone. Collect money.

## Stars Who Skimp

If these celebs can cut back, you can, too . . . .

- *Desperate Housewives* star Terri Hatcher drives an old VW bus.
- Tyra Banks buys cheap makeup from the drugstore.
- Sarah Michelle Gellar admits that she shops at Bloomingdale's on double reward days.
- Harrison Ford is worth about $300 million but still takes advantage of the senior discount when he goes to the movies.

# >>> 54. Your favorite beauty product has been discontinued

*Vogue* editor Anna Wintour has had the same haircut for 100 years. What if all of a sudden they ran out of scissors that cut bangs? It'd be a tragedy! Likewise, you've been using the same lipstick, eye shadow, all that stuff, for years and you look like a porcelain goddess because of it. But now because of the dang recession, your favorite beauty products have disappeared off the shelves. How can you go on living without your staples—air, water, food, and foundation?

## The OMG! solution to avoiding change

### → STEP #1: Go online

There are a ton of websites that carry discontinued stuff, like *www.cosmeticsandmore.com*, *www.discount.makeup.com*, and *www.beautyencounter.com*.

### → STEP #2: Call the founder

If you can't find it online, stalk the owners of the company. No doubt they have boxes of the stuff piling up in their garage.

### → STEP #3: Make it yourself

If that doesn't work, go back to college and get a degree in chemistry and figure out how to create the product on your own.

## → STEP #4: Go au naturel

If you stink at science, just give up, become a hippie, and go without makeup. Grow your hair out, stop bathing and wearing underwear, and burn incense. Listen to Peter, Paul, and Mary and drop acid. Protest the war and spit on veterans and call them baby killers. Wear tie-dye. Move to San Francisco. Have lots of sex with lots of different partners. Have a baby and name it Sparrow.

### In the Future...

68 percent of British men prefer that women have the fresh-faced look over looking like Bozo the Clown, dating website Loopylove.com's recent poll found.

### OMGesus!

Before the recession, women spent an average of $100 per month on beauty products and services, says a study from the YWCA. These days, a survey by DailyMakeover.com says, 44 percent are coloring their own hair, 76 percent are plucking their own eyebrows, and 86 percent are doing their own manicures.

## 55. Asian ladies make fun of you in Korean during a manicure

**Y**ou go to the salon to relax and look pretty. But as soon as you pick out your polish and sit down in one of those giant massage chairs, the chatter starts. Your pedicurist is having a snide conversation with another pedicurist—and you're pretty sure it's about you because they both keep looking at your feet and laughing. You'll never know, of course, as they are speaking Korean.

## The OMG! solution to deciphering a foreign language

### → OPTION #1: Pretend you understand

Butt into the conversation by laughing at what they say, too. They'll think you speak Korean and shut up.

### → OPTION #2: Use a tape recorder

Place it down by your feet and turn it on. She'll have no idea what you're doing and in her confusion, will opt to stay quiet and not chit-chat at all. If she asks, say you are taking a Korean class and want to use their banter for an assignment.

### → OPTION #3: Bring a friend

Talk in a made-up language and make it obvious you are talking about your cosmetologist. Who cares if an eye for an eye makes the whole world blind!

## → OPTION #4: Get her wet

When it's time to switch feet, "accidentally" kick water in her face. Then apologize profusely.

## → OPTION #5: Tip well

Listen, if you give them lots of money they are less likely to be rude in the future.

### OMGesus!

Florida, California, and New York have the most unlicensed nail salons. In South Florida, the same inspectors who check out nail salons inspect veterinarian offices! Experts suggest you bring your own tools.

### Is Your Nail Salon Unsanitary?

Look for these signs:

- There are pools of cloudy gray water in the jet baths.
- The technicians keep gagging.
- The tools have other people's toenail crud on them.

- The polish looks like it's been there since 1972.
- Your nails turn brown or green or disintegrate.
- You get hepatitis or flesh eating disease, or your toe has to be amputated.
- The pumice stones are actually just rocks from the parking lot.
- There's a cat walking around.

### Star Sighting

Paula Abdul says she got a thumb infection after going to a skanky salon in L.A.

*In the Future...*

Don't shave your legs before you get a pedicure. Nicks and cuts from shaved legs can make you more susceptible to infection!

## 56. You're treated like a criminal

**J**ust like Julia Roberts in *Pretty Woman*, you can't go into an upscale boutique without feeling like a second-class citizen. While you browse, the snotty saleswomen either ignore you or follow you around like you're gonna steal everything. Just because you're wearing cargo shorts and a T-shirt doesn't mean you're poor. Your generation spends $629 billion a year shopping. How do they know you're not going to plunk down a black American Express card?

## The OMG! solution to dealing with haughty couture

→ **STEP #1: Acknowledge your own existence**

Stand in the middle of the store and shout, "My father is a yogurt magnate and I have a giant trust fund. Who wants a nice commission?"

→ **STEP #2: Try everything on**

Don't be intimidated. Make them run around and bring you every dress on the rack.

→ **STEP #3: Be a diva**

Ask them for a glass of champagne and for lunch to be catered in.

## →STEP #4: Fake it

Bring a pile of clothes up to the register and after the rude worker rings it all up, take a credit card out and say, "I've changed my mind. I don't feel like shopping today."

### →STEP #5: Make a dramatic exit

Walk out backwards with your middle fingers in the air.

### You Are Also a Label Ho!

Your favorite brands, by Outlaw Consulting:

Apple

Trader Joe's

Jet Blue

In-N-Out Burger

Ben & Jerry's

Adidas

American Apparel

Target

H&M

Levi's

Volkswagen

Vitamin Water

# 57. You're spotted buying a pregnancy test

**Y**our monthly bill is late so, in panic, you head down to the local drugstore to pick up a pregnancy test. You're wearing a giant hat and Jackie O sunglasses so nobody will recognize you, but as you're walking toward the cashier, you're intercepted by a familiar face—your mom's best friend. As visions of dirty diapers, spit up, and your mother's cries of "Where did I go wrong?!" dance in your head, you must contain this potentially disastrous situation.

## The OMG! solution to keeping her quiet

### → OPTION #1: Act normal

There is a chance that if you act like absolutely nothing weird is happening, she won't notice the EPT box hidden under the Chia Pet and *In Touch Weekly* in your basket. It's unlikely, though, because people are inherently nosy. She'll probably sneak a glance at your stuff and see what's what.

### → OPTION #2: Maintain eye contact

If you look her in the eye without blinking, almost hypnotizing her, she might not look anywhere else but back in your eyes. Whatever you do, don't look down, because then her eyes will follow yours and she'll see that you might have gotten knocked up.

### → OPTION #3: Beg

If the jig is up, you could try pleading with her not to tell your parents. Hopefully, this woman is not the town gossip, in addition to being your mother's closest confidante.

> "He who gossips with you will gossip of you."
>
> —FROM A CHINESE FORTUNE COOKIE

### → OPTION #4: Bribe her

Is she cheating on her husband? Is her son secretly a drug dealer? Pull out whatever weapons you have in your arsenal and threaten to use them mercilessly.

## OMGesus!

A new Gallup poll shows that 51 percent of Americans say they are pro-life.

### → OPTION #5: Confide in her

You could try this route if you know she's competitive with your mom: Ask her to go for coffee and make her feel like she's the only one on earth you can trust. People like to feel special. If she thinks you covet her opinion and counsel, she may keep her big trap shut and be your secret mentor.

## More Embarrassing Things for Your Shopping Cart

All are available at *www.shopinprivate.com*:

Condoms

Douches

Hemorrhoid cream

Taylor Hicks CDs

KY Jelly

Anal bleaching cream

Enema bags

Dexatrim

Wart remover

Lice comb

Beano fart pills

Orgasmix Orgasm Enhancing Drops

Fart Filter Underwear Insert

Femtone Vaginal Weights

## 58. You pay $400 for a tattoo that is total gibberish

**Y**ou've always wanted a tattoo but couldn't decide what you'd like on your body for eternity. But then one day it came to you in a vision. You wanted the Japanese symbol for "Respect" on your forearm. After suffering through the process, which hurt like a son of a biscuit, you were so happy with your new body art and felt like such a hipster. But then one day, a wise old Asian man stopped you on the street and informed you that your tattoo actually means "cow pie."

### The OMG! solution for dealing with a dumb tattoo

→ **OPTION #1: Have it removed**

It'll cost a fortune and still never look right again, but it could give you peace of mind.

→ **OPTION #2: Fix it**

Hire Angelina Jolie's tattoo artist. Bet he never makes mistakes.

→ **OPTION #3: Turn it into something else**

Johnny Depp turned his Winona Ryder tribute tattoo "Winona Forever" into "Wino Forever."

→ **OPTION #4: Never wear short sleeves again**

Become a devout Muslim or orthodox Jew, because women

of those religions always have to cover their arms and legs.

### → OPTION #5: Have your arm amputated

Okay, you're not going to do this, but you really want to, don't you? How could you be so stupid!

### → OPTION #6: Get another one

The distraction will make you forget about your mistake, at least for a few minutes. It's like when you have a headache but then stub your toe. You forget about

the headache for a moment while you hobble around in pain cursing like a truck driver.

### Celebrity Tattoo Horror Stories

- David Beckham's Sanskrit tattoo spells his own wife's name wrong! Instead of reading "Victoria," it says "Vihctoria."
- Britney Spears had a kabbalah tattoo removed from the back of her neck after she decided she was bored with the mystical Jewish religion.
- *Heroes* star Hayden Panettiere showed off a new tattoo written in Italian all down her side in Cannes while sunbathing on a boat. It was supposed to mean "to live without regrets," but an extra letter changed the meaning to "to live without regretted." Oops.
- Rihanna's Sanskrit tattoo is supposed to say "forgiveness, honesty, suppression and control" but it's misspelled, too.

## OMGesus!

Women with large visible tattoos are more likely to be perceived as ugly, stupid liars than women with no tattoos, according to a study by Brookdale Community College. And by the way, 17 percent of people with tattoos regret getting them!

# 59. You witness your friend shoplifting

**Y**ou and a pal go to the mall together to browse and binge on pretzel dogs. But while you're in Hot Topic, you notice your friend slip a pair of cheap earrings into her purse. Minutes later, she hijacks an arm warmer and throws that in her bag, too. You are so stunned, you're speechless. She's a total klepto. Now what the heck do you do?

## The OMG! solution for dealing with a friend who has sticky fingers

→ **OPTION #1: Turn her in**

That way, when she goes to jail for eight months, you can steal her hot boyfriend.

→ **OPTION #2: Wish her a happy birthday!**

According to ShopliftingPrevention.org, many thieves shoplift on their birthdays as a little reward for themselves. After you successfully dodge the security guards, take her out for a steak and shrimp dinner at Benihana.

→ **OPTION #3: Hire her to bootleg movies, too**

She's already going to burn in hell, so why not make some money off of her in the meantime? Send her to new movies with a camcorder, then sell the grainy bootlegs on a street corner.

### → OPTION #4: Go on a crime spree

You know, like in *Thelma and Louise*. Rob some cute guys and shoot guns at horny truck drivers. Then drive off a cliff together and die.

## OMGesus!

In a covert University of Florida study of a drugstore in Atlanta, closed-circuit security cameras caught 8 percent of customers getting a five-finger discount! By the way, 70 percent of shoplifters are men, says criminologist Paul Cromwell from Wichita State University.

## Famous Shoplifters

**Bai Ling** *($16 worth of tabloid magazines and batteries)*

**Winona Ryder** *($4,760 worth of clothes and accessories from Saks)*

**Courtney Love** *(a Kiss T-shirt from Woolworth's)*

**Farrah Fawcett** *(clothes from boutiques)*

**Jennifer Capriati** *(a ring from a mall)*

**Rosario** *from Will & Grace ($400 in "tacky jewelry" from a department store)*

## Top Stolen Items

- Meat
- Pregnancy tests
- Alleve and Advil
- Razors
- Film
- Formula
- Preparation H
- Primatine tablets (to make meth perhaps?)

# 60. You accidentally break something

You're walking around a high-end store, looking at stuff you could never even think of buying. All of a sudden, you trip on the carpet and go flying into a display of ceramic goods. An expensive vase crashes on the ground and you are mortified. Plus, you're poor. How in the world are you going pay for this?

## The OMG! solution for fixing what IS broke

### → OPTION #1: Lie

When the salespeople come running over, tell them a little kid broke the vase and ran away. Point to nothing outside and say, "There's the little monster!" and run out as fast as you can.

### → OPTION #2: Threaten to sue

Be proactive. Tell the manager that the carpet was very dangerous and could have seriously injured you. Pretend to call Nancy Grace on your cell phone.

### → OPTION #3: Go blind

Quickly put your sunglasses on and stare straight ahead. It might help if you stretch out your arms like you're feeling around for objects in front of you. No person in their right mind would charge a visually impaired person for breaking something.

In the Future...

Break stuff on purpose at Sarah's Smash Shack (*www.smashshack.com*) in San Diego. At this shop, you can pay ten bucks to intentionally throw plates and/or glasses against the wall as hard as you can to relieve stress or frustrations.

### → OPTION #4: Act like a rock star

Tell the store that you broke it on purpose because you are a famous singer in a band called Suicide Corpse Destroyer and your manager will be by soon to pay for the damage.

## OMGesus!

Clumsy children are more likely to become obese adults by the age of thirty-three, the *British Medical Journal* reports. But another ridiculous study finds that if you're a smart kid, you're more likely to be a less clumsy adult.

# Chapter 7

# Keep Your
# Frienemies Close

OMG!

# >> 61. Your archenemy always tells you "You look tired. . . ."

Y ou're in a great mood, skipping down the street, when you run into the one girl in this world you can't stand. She's always so competitive with you and saying the rudest things to your besties. So, of course, after giving each other fake air kisses, she steps back, gives you the once-over, and blurts out, "You look tired. Are you okay?" Not anymore! Apparently you look like crap.

## The OMG! solution to dealing with passive-aggressive bee-yotches

### → OPTION #1: Feign illness

Tell her, no, in fact, you are not okay. You have just been diagnosed with a life-threatening, contagious disease and only have twenty-seven minutes to live. Cough and sneeze on her. Give her a giant hug and hold on tight. Wipe your nose on her shoulder so she believes she will catch it and die.

### → OPTION #2: Make her feel bad about herself

Say, "I know! I was up all night with [fill in name of her boyfriend]! We didn't get much sleep, if you know what I mean."

### → OPTION #3: Agree

Tell her she's right, you do look like shit because you've been partying too much. You should probably go to rehab or check yourself into a mental hospital for exhaustion.

## → OPTION #4: Give it right back

Thank her profusely for pointing your flaws out. Tell her that they both have been burning the candle at both ends and she doesn't look so good herself. Suggest that she get plastic surgery to fix those suitcases parked out under her eyes.

## → OPTION #5: Clock her

That's right. Punch her in the head. You know you've always wanted to.

### The Eyes Have It

Save your money! When researchers at Yale showed people pictures of faces that mimicked eyelid surgery or brow lifts, those faces were rated as looking sad and tired! And crow's feet were perceived as happiness!

## OMGesus!

In a Clinique survey, 53 percent of women said under-eye circles and puffiness were their #1 beauty concern.

### Stars That Really Do Look Tired

Amy Winehouse

Susan Boyle

Matthew Perry

Droopy Dog

Hillary Clinton

Harrison Ford

Lindsay Lohan

## >> 62. Your friend keeps stealing your style

**A**t first you were flattered when your pal kept saying how much she liked your clothes and how fashion forward you are. But then you made the mistake of taking her shopping with you. And the next thing you know, she looks exactly like you and even has some of the same outfits! We know what comes next—we've all seen *Single White Female*. Getting the same haircut, sleeping with your boyfriend, and trying to kill you in the basement of an apartment building with a stiletto. To avoid this situation, here are some ideas.

## The OMG! solution to dealing with a wardrobe copycat

### → OPTION #1: Wear weird things

Throw her off your trail. Tell her mom-jeans, leg warmers, and giant shoulder pads are in. Then point your finger and laugh at her as she's walking down the street. That'll teach her.

### → OPTION #2: Change your look

Does Madonna or Kate Moss only have one look? Hell no! They mix it up. So as soon as your friend mimics you, move on to the next best thing. Which you'll find in *In Style* or *Harper's Bazaar*.

## → OPTION #3: File a restraining order

She's obviously a danger to you and to society. Make sure she's not allowed to text or IM you or come within 500 feet of you.

## → OPTION #4: Embrace it

Obviously you are a leader and the people around you are a bunch of sheep. So start your own cult, where everyone dresses like you and worships you. Ask Tom Cruise to join and fund it.

### OMGesus!

A study at Brock University in Canada found that girls just can't win when it comes to fashion. According to researcher Rebecca Raby, they are expected to wear sexy popular fashions, but if they show too much cleavage or skin—they risk being called a slut!

### Top Ten Worst Fashion Trends in History

Mullets

Fanny packs

Stirrup and/or hammer pants

Acid-washed anything

Tie-dye

Socks and sandals

Parachute pants

Bike shorts

Holiday sweaters

Scrunchies

# 63. Your anorexic pal keeps tabs on what you eat

**Y**ou are normal. So when you are hungry, you put food in your mouth, swallow it and let it travel from your stomach to your bowels. But you have one emaciated acquaintance who is totally jealous because her diet consists of edamame, Diet Coke, and Marlboro Lights. And she constantly tries to make you feel guilty for ingesting anything at all. Say you're eating a pizza, and she'll say something like, "You're getting extra cheese? Wow, if I did that my ass would get so fat." It's this kind of talk that's making mealtimes unenjoyable. It must stop. There's only one way to handle this, and it's simple. You'll just have to eat the crappiest crap with abandon in front of her in order to turn her back into an eater.

## The OMG! list of diet-defying foods that will definitely make a famished friend eat again

### → OPTION #1: Cinnabons

Mmm, fresh baked goods. Just looking at one of these gooey treats can add an inch to your waistline but it's worth it. The icing is heavenly.

### → OPTION #2: Raw cookie dough

Whip up a batch of Toll House and lick the beaters in front of her. Then take a spoon and eat directly out of the mixing bowl.

When the saliva drips from her mouth to the floor, hand her an extra spoon.

### OMGesus!

10 percent of adolescent girls binge-eat or purge, according to the a report in *Pediatric and Adolescent Medicine*.

### → OPTION #3: Bacon

The pork product is a gift from God. Be sure to cook it in front of her. The sizzle and the smell should put her into a swine-induced trance.

### → OPTION #4: Movie popcorn with extra butter

For maximum enjoyment, go to the theater see a flick and get one of those giant tubs. Douse it in salt and squirt tons of butter all over it. Also buy some Milk Duds and eat those with the popcorn.

### → OPTION #5: McDonald's French fries

Anyone who doesn't like these is a wankstain.

### Weight Watching

This is how girls fourteen to twenty-two stay slim, according to a study by Growing Up Today at Harvard Medical School:

- 19 percent skip meals
- 23 percent limit portion size
- 24 percent eat a low-calorie diet
- 33 percent eat no dessert

## 64. Your ugliest friend calls dibs on every hot guy

You have a friend, who, shall we say, has a face made for radio. Beautiful on the inside, maybe not so much on the outside. Bottom line—she's fugly. And yet, to make up for her shortcomings, she has the biggest personality of all of the girls in your group. And whenever you all go somewhere, like a party or a club, she immediately stakes a claim on the hottest guy in the room. And he doesn't even want her! But you'll look like a slut and a bitch if you steal him away from her.

### The OMG! solution to dealing with a hottie hog

#### → OPTION #1: Set up a challenge

You should all have to compete like in a reality TV challenge to see who gets the guy. One time on an episode of the *Real World/ Road Rules Challenge*, all of the contestants had to lie in coffins and whoever could do it the longest without suffocating won. You should do that.

#### → OPTION #2: Take turns

It's only fair that you all switch off getting a first crack at the stud.

#### → OPTION #3: Stop inviting her

Find some great excuses to leave her behind. Always travel in the smallest car possible and tell her there's no room. If you're going out for dinner say you can't change the reservation and add more people. Tell her you'll meet her there an hour later than you actually show up.

### → OPTION #4: Sabotage her

Pull the guy aside and tell him that she really wants to get married and have kids right away. That's all she ever talks about.

### → OPTION #5: Steal him anyway

Here's the rule: If he didn't buy her a drink, get her phone number, or kiss her, he's fair game. Go for it and deal with the fallout later.

## OMGesus!

Remember, ho's before bro's! According to an Australian study by Flinders University, people who had a large network of friends out-lived those with the fewest friends by 22%--and the study is legit, it followed nearly 1,500 older people for 10 years. That's a long time.

### More Reasons We Need Friends

- Women with more friends lived 22 percent longer than women with fewer friends.
- A study at the Universite du Quebec at Montreal, Harvard University, and Emmanuel College in Boston found that women were more likely than men to sever a friendship after a single offense.

## 65. Your friend is a major name-dropper

**S**o, your new pal is like the opposite of Annie Wilson on *90210*. She lived in L.A. her whole life, but recently moved to your Podunk town when her dad got transferred. Now, she likes to think her shit don't stank—and she loves to brag about hanging out with everyone from Zac Efron to Drew Barrymore. Every time she opens her mouth, she says something like, "This one time, when I was chillin' with Lindsay and Sam back in Hollywood . . . ." It's totally obnoxious—and probably all lies anyway!

### The OMG! solution to dealing with a fame-whoring boaster

→ **OPTION #1: Play dumb**

Bragger: *"Britney and I took a dance class together."*

You: *"Who's Britney?"*

Bragger: *"Spears!"*

You: [blank look]

Bragger: *"You don't know who Britney Spears is?"*

You: *"She's that singer, right? Yeah, I'm not really into opera though."*

## → OPTION #2: Wander off topic

**Bragger:** *"Nicole and Joel throw the best dinner parties."*

**You:** *"Speaking of dinner, I'm so hungry. What should I eat tonight? I was thinking Mexican."*

**Bragger:** *"Nicole and Joel once made Churros. It was awesome!"*

**You:** *"Mexican gives me gas. I think I'll have Thai food. Have you tried that new place on 43rd? They have amazing spring rolls."*

## OMGesus!

- 31 percent of teenagers believe they'll be famous one day, says a study by *Psychology Today*.
- 43.4 percent of teenage girls want to be the personal assistant to a celebrity when they grow up versus being a U.S. senator or the CEO of a company like General Motors, according to research at Syracuse University.
- More teenagers would rather have dinner with Paris Hilton than Jesus Christ.

## → OPTION #3: Steal her thunder

**Bragger:** *"John Mayer asked for my phone number on Twitter."*

**You:** *"I don't feel well. Oh no, I think I'm going into diabetic shock. Someone call an ambulance!"*

## → OPTION #4: Make her feel shallow

**Bragger:** *"Brad and Angelina are so much better-looking in person."*

**You:** *"I want to adopt a baby from Namibia, too. After that, I want to build a hospital in Malawi and start a school for girls in Darfur. I could use your help. Do you want to join my committee?"*

## In the Future...

The best ways to meet a celebrity are:

Going to rehab

Becoming a paparazzi

Getting hired as a nanny

Pretending you're dying and signing up for Make-A-Wish

Moonlighting as a high-class hooker in Hollywood

Practicing your BJ skills and becoming a groupie

# 66. Your BFF spills your deepest, darkest secret

**A**fter you cheated on your boyfriend, you were so racked with guilt, you had to confess your dirty deed to someone. So after pinky-swearing with your friend, you sent her the e-mail love letters you got from the new guy and asked her advice. She vowed that she would never tell—cross her heart, hope to die, stick a needle in her eye. But then, one day, you guys got into a heated fight over who's hotter, Chace Crawford or Ed Westwick. And that argument exploded into World War III, and resulted in you calling her selfish and insecure. The next thing you know, she's forwarded the incriminating evidence to your soon-to-be-ex.

## The OMG! solution for getting revenge on a big mouth

### → OPTION #1: Post anonymous things about her online

Gandhi said, "An eye for an eye makes the whole world blind," but screw that. If she's going to spill your secrets, you should spill hers. Tell everyone about that weird mole she has on her butt that looks like a poo stain!

### → OPTION #2: Put a horse head in her bed

In *The Godfather*, when this one guy didn't do what this Mafia guy wanted, the Mafia guy put a dead horse head in his bed. And the guy wakes up screaming hysterically.

### →OPTION #3: Sign her up for dirty magazine subscriptions

It won't really do anything, other than make you really happy.

## OMGesus!

According to Anita E. Kelly in the book *The Psychology of Secrets*, research has shown that the top three secrets people usually keep to themselves are about sex, mental health, and failure!

### →OPTION #4: Use a poison pen

When she's not looking, write "Rat" on her coat with an ultraviolet marker. So when she's in a dark club it'll show up.

> " *I don't keep secrets because I'm no good at it. I have a big mouth. If you were my friend, I'd tell you not to tell me a secret, like who you have a crush on.*"
>
> —MILEY CYRUS

**Most Trustworthy Celeb Girlfriends, According to *Forbes***

Oprah

Sandra Bullock

Rachael Ray

Jennifer Aniston

# 67. Your friend is a pathological liar

ately you notice that everything that comes out of your friend's mouth is a little too good to be true. She aced her SATs, even though she's kind of dumb. You hear her telling her mom that she stayed at your place last night and you guys knitted, when you know for a fact she was out the night before until 3 A.M.—and not at your house. She lies about anything and everything, from the kind of toothpaste she uses to how much money she has in the bank. You just don't know if you can believe one word that comes out of her mouth anymore. What happened to her? It's time to call her out on it.

## The OMG! solution to spotting a fibber

### → STEP #1: Look

Liars often have forced smiles, trouble making eye contact, and dilated pupils, and they blink a lot. They also fidget, cover their face with their hand, and turn sideways when they're fibbing.

### → STEP #2: Listen

Liars complain a lot, pause a lot, leave out details, and give generic details. Also, does her voice go up an octave suddenly when she's bragging about the fabulous party she went to? If it does, she could be making it up.

## → STEP #3: Play detective

Think about the stuff your friend is saying. Does it really add up or are there as many holes as Swiss cheese in her stories? Make the friend tell the story over again and look for inconsistencies.

## → STEP #4: Confront

Don't be like, "Gotcha!" Just calmly present the facts. The shame will make the liar stop lying so much, at least to you.

### OMGesus!

21 percent of IM messages contain a lie. And people lie in face-to-face conversations 27 percent of the time, according to a Cornell University study called "Deception and Design: The Impact of Communication on Lying Behavior."

## You Lie Like a Rug

According to a study on fibbing at the University of Massachusetts, 60 percent of the participants lied three times during a ten-minute conversation! Women are more likely to lie to make another person feel good, while men tend to lie to make themselves look better.

### In the Future...

You should make up stuff. Research at the University of Massachusetts shows that good liars are more popular.

## 68. Your BFF went MIA as soon as she got a boyfriend

**Y**ou've been tight with your BFF since the second grade. You weathered cooties, puberty, and PSATs together. You went to the same college because you couldn't stand the idea of being apart, and you've been roommates forever. Nobody gets you like she does—and nobody has ever come between you. But then recently she met this stupid guy and he's swiftly taken your place. He's her new best friend and shoulder to cry on. You rarely see her anymore because she's always over at his place. But every time you do meet up with her, she drags him along and he just sits there like an oaf. Suddenly, you're always the third wheel and feel like you're imposing on their together time.

### The OMG! solution to dealing with being the third wheel

**→ OPTION #1: Bring a posse**

Don't ever be alone with them, or you'll have to suffer through pet names and PDA's. If she's going to bring her ball and chain everywhere you go, just show up everywhere with your most obnoxious friends, too, unannounced.

**→ OPTION #2: Make her jealous**

Make the most exciting plans in the world with only your girlfriends and don't invite her. Afterwards, brag about how fun it was. When she says that she wants to come next time, say, "Yeah, sorry, but it's a girls' night out and you always bring [OAF'S NAME] wherever you go."

### → OPTION #3: Alienate him

Start planning events that she must come to that you know he will not enjoy. Like pedicures for someone's birthday. Or facials to celebrate another pal's promotion.

## OMGjesus!

If you can't beat 'em, join 'em. About 23 percent of adults have admitted to having had a threesome, a Playboy survey found!

### → OPTION #4: Have a threesome

Get drunk and seduce them both. After you all have sexual relations, it will all be so awkward that they will end up breaking up and then you'll get your best friend back.

## In the Future...

As soon as they break up—and they will—she's going to want to be your instant BFF again. But she'll need to get back in your good graces first. Here are some things she should be required to do first:

- Write a poem about the true meaning of friendship.
- Buy a star and name it after you.
- Bring you lots of donuts.
- Give you a back massage every week for two months.

# 69. You're not invited to the best party of the year

Everyone can't stop talking about the biggest bash of the year. It's at the hottest club in town, it's an open bar, and The Kooks are playing for free. Here's the rub. The wench throwing the party is your boyfriend's ex. She believes, wrongly, that you stole him away from her. So even though your beau is invited, she's left you off the guest list on purpose!

## The OMG! solution to crashing a party

### → OPTION #1: Go in disguise

Dress up like a man. Then hit on the hostess at the party. Make sure you make out with her on the dance floor so everyone sees. Then, like in *Just One of the Guys*, one of the best movies ever, do a big reveal where you take off your costume, lift up your shirt and show everyone that you are girl! Laugh maniacally and walk out.

### → OPTION #2: Pretend you belong

Just show up anyway as if you were invited. Bring a gift and be sweet as pie to the hostess, even though you hate her. If she thinks you're totally clueless that you weren't invited, she's less likely to throw your ass out.

### → OPTION #3: Show up late

The drunker the hostess is, the more unable she'll be to see you clearly. Or she could be totally belligerent and smash a wine bottle over your head. So be prepared for either situation to occur.

### → OPTION #4: Invite others

Post an open invitation to it on MySpace and Facebook. One time rock star Annie Lennox's kid did that and so many people crashed the party, her mansion was totally destroyed!

## OMGesus!

Post-collegiate coeds party the hardest, and drink dangerous amounts of booze, according to a study by the National Institute on Alcohol Abuse and Alcoholism, but they're also the most health-conscious—they smoke less, eat organic foods, and exercise!

### → OPTION #5: Call the cops

Make an anonymous call from a phone booth and say that Osama bin Laden has been spotted at the shindig.

*"I don't like parties past 2 A.M. Then it's all losers and weirdoes."*

—PARIS HILTON

# 70. Your boyfriend cheats on you with your BFF

You are the last one to know. According to another frienemy, one of your closest pals has been secretly seeing your boyfriend behind your back. You expect it from him, because he's a jerk. But how could she? When you confront her, she says she didn't want to tell you because she knew you'd freak out. She's right. You're freaking out! Not cool. And now that you know, they feel it's okay to flaunt their love openly. So, whenever you see them together, you want to puke.

## The OMG! solution to when you see the happy f@%$ing couple together

### → STEP #1: Be immature

A lot of people would say, stay calm, be an adult. But that's how wimps get walked all over like a doormat. You should be like, "Well, well. If it isn't Brad and Angelina! I suppose I'm Jennifer Aniston in this situation. Guess what? Jennifer Aniston makes more money than Angelina Jolie— and she's got better hair. Have fun making a soccer team together!"

### → STEP #2: Talk a lot

They'd probably like it if you'd just ignore them so they don't have to deal. No way, they're not getting off that easy. Talk to them about everything under the sun. It'll make them beyond uncomfortable.

## → STEP #3: Point out his flaws

Just so your friend knows she got sloppy seconds, rattle off statistics about your ex's performance while hooking up. Like, "Does he do that thing with his mouth on the earlobe still? Yeah, that felt pretty good but he'll do that a lot. He's not very creative."

## → STEP #4: Linger

They want you to go away as soon as possible. Don't. Stay there until the sun comes up if you have to.

> ## OMGesus!
>
> According to a Public Opinion Strategies poll in *Cosmopolitan* magazine, 50 percent of single men still pine over an old flame, compared to just 27 percent of single women.

> *"It is better to have a relationship with someone who cheats on you than with someone who does not flush the toilet."*
>
> —UMA THURMAN

## → STEP #5: Make out with a stranger

Make your ex jealous. Find the hottest guy in the room and shove your tongue in his mouth. Sure, you might look a little desperate but it will prove that you've moved on.

# Online E-diots

# >> 71. Google your name and you see "BEEF CURTAINS"

There isn't a soul on earth who hasn't Googled him- or herself (except maybe your grandparents). But what happens when mean girls, a competitive coworker, or a jilted ex sullies your reputation by writing scandalous and occasionally untrue gossip about your sexual secrets and stimulant intake? It's important to get rid of that stuff—because it's very likely that future employers and boyfriends will Google you. And nobody wants to hire or date a stoned hussy.

## The OMG! solution to fixing your online reputation

→ **STEP #1: Sign up for Google Alerts**

Any time someone spreads rumors about you, you will be notified.

→ **STEP #2: Start a blog or a website called *www.yourname .com***

If you have your own blog, that will pop up first in a Google search and the other stuff will get buried. Update your blog often with fresh content, which will ensure that it's the top line of the Google search.

→ **STEP #3: Sign up for every social site**

Get on Twitter, Flickr, YouTube, Digg, Facebook . . . . The more accounts you have, the more of that first page they'll take up and then that picture of you making out with a homeless man will get bumped to the second page.

## → STEP #4: If all else fails and you still look like a big slut, hire an online reputation management firm.

Companies like ReputationDefender and Naymz can reshape your online image for a few thousand bucks. So even if you are a drunken hussy, these guys will make you seem as innocent as Mother Teresa!

### OMGjesus!

37 percent of Americans have admitted to being filmed naked, says an *Adam & Eve* survey. 22 percent of Australian women admit to having made a sex tape, according to the book *Sex Lives of Australian Women* by Joan Sauers.

### Don't Do This, or It'll End Up Online

- Make your eyes look Chinese, like Miley Cyrus did.
- Grab a cardboard cutout of Hillary Clinton's boob, like Barack Obama's head speechwriter did.
- Tell racist jokes at a comedy club, like Michael "Kramer" Richards did.
- Scream profanities at an underling, like Christian "Batman" Bale did.
- Call your daughter "a little pig" in a voicemail, like Alec Baldwin did.

### How to Make a Safe Sex Tape (if you must)

1. Keep your face hidden.
2. Cover identifiable characteristics, like moles and tattoos.
3. Keep it in a locked place.
4. Don't tell anyone about it.
5. Don't throw it away without destroying it.

## 72. Your boyfriend won't change his status to "in a relationship"

**Y**ou've been dating your significant other for six months. He's met your friends, your family, and your coworkers. You've had the discussion about being exclusive and know that you are madly in love. And still, he refuses to do one small thing that will make you infinitely happy—he won't change his status on MySpace and Facebook to "committed" or "taken" or "in a relationship." What the F? One of the greatest moments in life is being able to brand your online profiles with "in a relationship." It's what every girl dreams of!

### The OMG! solution to convincing your mate to make the commitment

→ **STEP #1: Change your status to "Single" or "It's complicated"**

When your boyfriend sees the cute little shattered red heart, he will become alarmed and wonder if he's made the biggest mistake of his life not bending to your whims.

→ **STEP #2: Flirt with a friend**

Make him jealous. Publicly wall-banter back-and-forth with the hottest guy in your Friend List.

→ **STEP #3: Post sexy pics**

Take naughty photos and "accidentally" put them in your photo albums.

### → STEP #4: Have friends write made-up comments

Ask your buddies to post comments about the wild night out you just had and ask if Sebastian the Brazilian model called you yet.

## OMGesus!

Promiscuous males are prone to diabetes and less able to handle stress, according to *Disease Models and Mechanisms*.

### → STEP #5: Make vague status updates

Post love poems by e.e. cummings, Keats, or Neruda. Your boyfriend will wonder if they are about him or Sebastian. He will come around. If he doesn't, screw him!

### The Best Cities for Single Women

If he doesn't come around, move to one of these towns to meet a new guy.

1. Chicago
2. Alexandria, Virginia
3. San Diego
4. Vancouver, B.C.
5. Raleigh, North Carolina

### Famous commitment-phobes

- George Clooney
- John Mayer
- George Costanza
- Hitler
- Derek Jeter
- Lance Armstrong

# 73. Your mother wants to be your friend on Facebook

There it is, sitting in your Inbox. You have a friend request—and it's from your mom. You absolutely don't want to accept her, because then you'll have to monitor every single word and picture you and your friends post, but you also don't want to hurt her feelings. Unfortunately, some of your brownnose buddies have already accepted her, making you look like a big jerk if you don't, too.

## The OMG! solution to avoiding an online friendship with a parent

### → STEP #1: Clean up your page

Before you let your mom in on your world, go through your profile with a fine-tooth comb. Get rid of any scandalous photos and references to drugs and/or underage drinking. Delete comments about you puking or hooking up or sneaking out of your house—or any other debaucherous behavior.

### → STEP #2: Accept her

After one last look-see, press the confirm button and write her a sweet message.

### → STEP #3: Create a new profile

Using a nickname or a pseudonym, make an entire new page for just your friends. Inform all of your pals quietly that you have a new profile. Update the other one every once in a while so your mom has no idea you have another page.

### → STEP #4: Make it private

Be sure to block anyone but close friends from being able to find your new profile. Then get back to being the crazy drunk slut your friends know and love.

*In the Future...*

A good trick to get rid of undesirables is to accept them as a friend, then delete them a few weeks later. They'll have so many friends and posts that they won't even realize you're missing!

Confirm Your Mother as a friend?

Accept

Deny

Block

# 74. Your niece keeps putting up family photos of you in your pajamas

The worst thing about the Internet is that you often have no control over what's said about you—and worse, what pictures people put up of you. And it's particularly maddening when a well-intentioned family member posts pics of you at the ugly preteen age of thirteen or at family gatherings, where you're wearing a hideous holiday sweater and have five double chins. Then you're tagged and 50,000 people see your disfigured face and body.

## The OMG! solution to ensuring that you are always taking good pictures

### → OPTION #1: Wear sunglasses

Jack Nicholson may be 136 years old but he always looks cool because he wears shades 24-7. You should do the same thing. Don't ever be photographed without them on.

### → OPTION #2: Control the angle

Never be in a picture unless the camera is above you. It sheds pounds.

### → OPTION #3: Practice your pose

Take a million Polaroids of your face until you find the one that makes you look hot. Then any time there is a camera around, plaster that look on for the duration.

### →OPTION #4: Only take pix with fat people

You, in comparison, will always look skinny.

### →OPTION #5: Eliminate old pictures

Visit all family members and go through their photo albums and delete or destroy every single ugly picture of yourself.

## OMGesus!

66 percent of women surveyed by Hewlett-Packard said they are "deeply embarrassed" by the way they look in pictures! And another study shows that eight out of ten women hate their reflection and more than half see a distorted image.

### In the Future...

Bring your camera everywhere you go and be in control of the picture-taking! That way, you can make yourself look good and everyone else look huge and greasy. Also, researchers at Cambridge University have found that nearly half of the social networking sites don't immediately delete pictures when a user requests they be removed. So stop doing stupid things and letting people take pictures of you!

# 75. Your friend updates his status, or Twitters, every five seconds

**M**ySpace, Facebook, and Twitter are swell but they've also created a nation of narcissists. Now, anyone with a pulse has a pulpit to write whatever's on his or her mind, such as "Dave: giggles every time President Obama talks about his stimulus package." (Okay, that one is actually kind of funny. Nice going, Dave.) But most updates are inane, pointless, mildly offensive, or just plain stupid. And they never end. There's always that one guy, cough cough John Mayer (see below), who thinks he needs to vomit his every waking thought. Listen, buddy, you don't. Nobody cares what you have to say.

## The OMG! solution to dealing with incessant— and unnecessary—tweets

→ **OPTION #1: Ignore it**

→ **OPTION #2: Direct tweet "you're an idiot"**

→ **OPTION #3: Start a terrible tweet-off**

Who can tweet more about less important stuff? Have your other friends judge (that's if they haven't stopped following you)

## OMGjesus!

Is anyone actually working anymore? MySpace has about 34 billion page views per month. Facebook has 20 billion. In the meantime, spam now accounts for 90.4 percent of all e-mail, according to Symantec.

## Totally Awesome (and Embarrassing) Status Update Topics

"Garry is masturbating!"

"Melissa just found out she has herpes!"

"Marianne is PMSing!"

"Paola is on lithium!"

"Liza thinks she might have been molested by a priest!"

## The Top 20 Most Annoying Status Updates Ever

1. "Thank God it's Friday! Can't wait for the weekend!"

2. Solicitations for money for charities

3. Serious health updates—inappropriate!

4. Political diatribes or pleas to be Green

5. Updates that go longer than two lines—about anything

6. Meatheads' brags about their workouts

7. "Bored at work"

8. Cute things kids did

9. Wedding planning updates

10. Counting down to an event nobody else is going to

11. Spoiling a TV show ending for the West Coast

12. Depression and defeatist sob stories, like, "Melvin: just can't do it anymore."

13. Esoteric BS, like "Sip and Twirl."

14. Obvious passive-aggressive subliminal messages to exes

15. Jet setters' boasts about their fabulous trips

16. Love notes between smug couples

17. Alcoholics' complaints about another hangover

18. Obscure song lyrics

19. Rooting for a local sports team

20. Pleas to come to your damn show for the four-hundredth time

| **OMG!** > Your friend updates his status, or Twitters, every five seconds

# 76. WebMD says you're dying

So you're feeling kind of weird, a bit under the weather, and decide to go to one of those Internet doctor sites to see if there's really something wrong with you. After answering all of the questions about your symptoms, like nausea and dizziness, you get some scary news—you appear to have a deadly disease and could possibly die by the next morning.

## The OMG! solution to getting freaky news on a medical website

### → STEP #1: Cry

Your first natural reaction when you find out you have hours to live is probably shock, then tears. Go ahead, let it out. Life is so cruel. You had such a promising future and now it's all being taken away from you.

### → STEP #2: Don't panic

The worst thing you can do in the last moments of your life is waste energy having an anxiety attack. You should grab a pen, make a Bucket List, and do all of the things you've ever dreamed of, like skydiving, learning how to speak Japanese, and meeting Prince Harry.

### → STEP #3: Be skeptical

Wait a minute. You know what? Maybe you're not dying. Is it possible that this website has given you the worst-case scenario? After all, you ate oysters tonight and they did smell really fishy. Maybe you just have food poisoning.

### → STEP #4: Get a second opinion

But not from just any old doctor! According to a recent study by Manhattan Research, 50 percent of physicians who go online for professional reasons use Wikipedia to answer health questions. Um, yeah, the same site that once reported that soccer god David Beckham was a Chinese beekeeper in the eighteenth century.

## OMGesus!

While 60 percent of peeps get medical information online, according to Opinion Research Corporation, 54 percent followed the advice they found. But 37 percent did not believe the advice they found.

### → STEP #5: Don't take life for granted

This experience has taught you a valuable lesson—life is a gift and should be cherished. Hug the people you love every day. Volunteer at a soup kitchen. You've been so selfish and now it's time to help others and share the knowledge you have gained. Don't waste time being angry. And never go on medical websites again.

" *There are many dying children out there whose last wish is to meet me.*"

—*DAVID HASSELHOFF*

# >>> 77. You're going broke from shopping online

**B**uying stuff online is so easy. Too easy. With just a scroll and a couple of clicks, beautiful boxes containing shoes, jewelry, and dresses arrive at your doorstep within days. There's only one problem with this. You actually have to pay for all of this crap. And you're maxing out your credit cards and can't make rent this month!

## The OMG! solution to avoiding bankruptcy

### → OPTION #1: Take a breather

When you're wigging out and putting a million things in your cart, step away from the computer. Go pluck your eyebrows or shave your legs and come back later to re-evaluate whether you really need both the Coach and the Louis Vuitton bags.

### → OPTION #2: Don't shop when you're smashed

Danger: Coming home from a night out all liquored up is a recipe for disaster. It's the online equivalent of drunk-dialing a guy. You wake up in the morning with major self-loathing and regret.

### → OPTION #3: Block sites

You could buy software that literally prevents you from going on certain sites. But you'd have to be a total addict for that to happen. Only 6 percent of people have some sort of online addiction, like porn or gambling, says a study by the American Psychological

Association, so it's probably not you. Yet.

### → OPTION #4: Get out of the house

The anonymity of online shopping in your undies makes it so seductive. Whereas if you actually had to get dressed, drive to the mall, wander around, try things on, and bring a big pile of stuff up to the counter, you might think twice about taking your credit card out of your purse.

## OMGesus!

Women buy an average of fourteen items of clothing each year—jeans, blouses, skirts, dresses, and shoes—that never leave the closet! And more than 33 percent buy clothes that are too small on purpose, hoping they will lose weight and eventually fit into them. Or so the Scottish company Lloydspharmacy found in a study.

*"Wal-Mart . . . do they like make walls there?"*

—PARIS HILTON

### Are you an eBay addict?

1. Would you rather get a rush from outbidding someone or doing loads of cocaine?
2. Do you schedule your life around vintage Easy-Bake Oven auctions?
3. Have you ever lied to people and not told them about your vintage Easy-Bake Oven collection?
4. Do you get irritable when there are no vintage Easy-Bake Ovens to bid on?
5. Have you ever skipped work to partake in an auction for vintage Easy-Bake Oven accessories?

## >>> 78. Your Internet date is a troll

**Y**our love life was in a rut. Everybody kept saying, "Try Internet dating, you'll like it! So-and-so met whatshername online! They're getting married!" So you took the plunge and signed up. You filled out your questionnaire as wittily as possible and posted the best picture you have of yourself. You got a ton of responses, and after weeding through the serial killers and child molesters, you came across a cute guy who seemed really awesome. You both liked tequila, *Mad Men*, and the *New York Times* crossword puzzle. You IM'd for a couple of weeks and had great conversations about life and love. So you finally set up a time and place to meet. On the day of the date, you're so excited, you get there early. But when Prince Charming walks in the door, he looks nothing like his photo. He's the size of Kevin Connolly, he's losing his hair, and his teeth are yellow. Plus he's wearing a vest. How in the world are you going to get out of this?

## The OMG! solution to ditching a dud

### → STEP #1: Drink up

Forget dinner. Just have a cocktail at the bar so you're not stuck with him for several hours.

### → STEP #2: The phony phone ring

Pretend your phone is vibrating. Answer and have a fake

conversation with a friend. Act shocked and say, "Oh no! What happened?"

## → STEP #3: Plan the escape

Tell rotten teeth that your aunt (use a relative that doesn't really exist for better karma) fell down and broke her hip. You have to go to the hospital.

## → STEP #4: Disappear

As soon as you get home, delete your profile. And while you're at it, get a new IM address, e-mail, and anything else that this guy might have.

### OMGesus!

Blondes have more disastrous than fun first dates. According to a British online dating service PARSHIP.co.uk, they are more likely to talk about ex-lovers, drink too much, and have sex with their date on the first night.

### From . . . MISMATCH.COM

- Female online daters are most likely to lie about their weight (59 percent), height (42 percent), and age (13 percent).
- Men lie most about their height (61 percent), weight (55 percent), and age (24 percent).
- Internet profiles also often contain lies about income, politics, education, and smoking habits, researchers at Cornell have found.
- The *Journal of the American Medical Association* found high rates of syphilis among people meeting online and having sex.

# >>> 79. Your boyfriend is addicted to Internet porn

**Y**our computer is on the fritz so you borrow your boyfriend's laptop. After you turn it on, you're really just planning on checking your e-mail. But you've always been a bit of a snoop. So you start checking out his folders and you come across one labeled "Photos." Thinking it might be your wonderful trip to the beach last summer, you open it. But instead of sand and surf, you see silicone and sex. Lots of sex.

## The OMG! solution to dealing with a porn-addicted partner

### → OPTION #1: Delete it

Dump the whole folder in the trash (make sure you take the extra step to then delete it again from the Recycle Bin or trash can) and replace it with photos of butterflies and rainbows. He'll likely flip out, but he's going to complain to whom exactly?

### → OPTION #2: Watch it

Of the 10 percent of Americans who are addicted to Internet porn, 28 percent of those are women. That could include you!

### → OPTION #3: Tell his mother

He'll be so mortified, he'll stop looking at porn. For a while at least. But he may also break up with you.

→ **OPTION #4: Take him to a shrink**, who will probably try to connect his porn addiction to the way his awful mother treated him as a child (see Option #3).

→ **OPTION #5: Dump him**

Regular porn users are more likely to go on drinking binges and more likely to have sex with multiple partners, says a study by those teetotalers at Brigham Young University.

## OMGjesus!

States that consume the most porn tend to be more conservative and religious, a study by Harvard Business School found.

→ **OPTION #6: Embrace it**

According to an ABC News *Primetime Live* sex survey, 52 percent of men under thirty have visited a sex website and 11 percent have participated in a sex chat room.

Even though 42 percent of women think visiting a porn site is cheating, it's inevitable. Why fight it?

> *"I am disappointed that my parents didn't give birth to a porn star."*
>
> —*RUFUS WAINWRIGHT*

### Porn to Be Wild

- Supermodel Christie Brinkley's husband Peter Cook had a $3,000 per month porn habit.
- *X-Files* star David Duchovny spent hours in sex chat rooms and had to go to sex addiction rehab.
- Red Hot Chili Peppers frontman Anthony Kiedis told *Blender* magazine, "I realized the feeling that I was having was like the feeling that I used to get when I'd go score drugs. I actually had to make a commitment to myself to stop."

Your pal thinks she's the second coming of Perez Hilton. She has a blog that she's always bragging about and forcing you to read. But here's the deal. According to anyone who has a pulse, 99 percent of the time, blogs are self-absorbed and boring. They are the equivalent of getting a friend's Christmas card letter—every day for the rest of your life. So you never read it, but she's always asking you, "What did you think of my blog today?" Then when it's obvious you haven't looked at it in like four months, she pouts.

## The OMG! best excuses for avoiding reading your friend's blog

### → OPTION #1: You have computer eyestrain

Tell her that lately you've been seeing spots, having dry eyes, and getting headaches after being on your computer all day. And you finally went to the doctor, and he told you that, like 50 percent of computer users, you have the terrible affliction of computer eyestrain. You're now supposed to only use your computer for work and/or school projects.

### → OPTION #2: You're creating your own blog

Mention that you are starting a website called PartyInMyPants.

com and that you don't want to read her blog because you don't want to be influenced by her content. Your blog must be pure and creatively unique.

### → OPTION #3: You're busy volunteering

Say that you are working long hours with a charity that helps female inmates adjust back into society. When she realizes that you are doing important work in the world, she'll stop insisting you read her mindless blather. Or maybe not.

### → OPTION #4: You've converted to Amish

They don't use technology because they feel it weakens the family structure. So you're not allowed to use your computer anymore. To prove it, start wearing bland brown clothing covered with a cape and an apron. Top off your outfit with a bonnet.

## OMGesus!

Bloggers are not just antisocial hermits sitting around in their pajamas. A study at Swinburne University found that people get more sociable and more self-confident after blogging.

## Word Up

"Blog" was added to the Oxford English Dictionary in 2005. Here are some other words that have recently been officially inducted into the same dictionary:

Bling bling (2003)

Crack ho' and hoochie (2004)

Wedgie (2005)

Unibrow, soul patch, and drama queen (2006)

Ginormous (2007)

Meh (2008)

# Chapter 9

# Bad Job

## >> 81. You have to poo but are too embarrassed

**Y**ou go out for lunch with your coworkers to that new Ethiopian restaurant. It's delicious but very rich and spicy. In the middle of the afternoon, you're sitting at your desk filing reports when you hear a strange rumble down below. All of a sudden your stomach is cramping and you're drenched in sweat. You realize if you don't make it to the bathroom ASAP, you might have a terrible accident. But there's another problem. You're not a guy. You can't just walk into the restroom with a newspaper and settle in for twenty minutes. You hate going Number Two in public places, especially at work! And this is going to be a doozy of a dump.

## The OMG! solution to pinching a loaf in public

→ **STEP #1: Choose wisely**

Pick the farthest stall down in the bathroom for some privacy.

→ **STEP #2: Send out a distress signal**

Hold off as long as possible until you have the bathroom alone.

Often, if you just sit there quietly at first, the other women can sense that you're having an issue, and they might hurry up and get the hell out. Because nobody wants to listen to another person lay cable. If it's a high-traffic bathroom, you'll just have to adjust.

### → STEP #3: Synchronize

To cover up your squirts, do it when others flush the toilet, turn on the hand dryer or wash their hands in the sink. Also, flush the toilet yourself often so that the poo smell doesn't have time to linger.

### → STEP #4: Wait for the next shift

To avoid embarrassing stares, don't leave until a new crop of women come into the bathroom. If they just got in there, they'll have no idea that you're the one who stunk up the joint.

### → STEP #5: Let it go

Remember, everyone poops. And think about it, do you specifically remember a time when someone else dropped off the kids at the pool? Of course not. So even if you're a little mortified now, it will all be forgotten.

## OMGesus!

On average, people go to the bathroom five times a day (once to poop and four times to pee), says the book *The Truth about Poop*.

### More Craptastic Facts

- Americans flush 108 million pounds of poop every day, according to *www.poopreport.com*.
- Spanish sailors once used the frayed end of old anchor ropes to wipe themselves.
- Boys poop their pants more often than girls.
- Snakes poop every ninety days.
- 75 percent of your poo is made of water, 33 percent is dead bacteria. Ew.

## Shit Happens

Ever notice that women's public restrooms are revolting? Women can be such animals. Here are some rules to live, learn, and love:

- Do not leave the plastic paper thing on the toilet seat! If you put it on, take it off!
- Discard feminine hygiene products in the bin.
- If you're going to hover over the seat instead of sitting down, wipe your damn pee splash off afterwards.
- Nobody cares that you love the environment. Flush the toilet!
- Do not talk on your cell phone in the stall. That's gross.

> *"Never kick a fresh turd on a hot day."*
>
> —PRESIDENT HARRY S. TRUMAN

# 82. Some a-hole warms fish in the microwave and other office offenses

**A**t the average place of employment, the kitchen is a biohazardous nest of bacteria. People leave their dirty dishes and coffee-stained mugs in the sink, let leftovers rot in the refrigerator for weeks, and the garbage can reeks like the city dump. They also steal other people's food. But perhaps the most disgusting thing to happen in the kitchen is what people choose to cook in the communal microwave. When some health-conscious wiener puts fish in there, it can stink up the whole office for the entire afternoon.

## The OMG! solution to dealing with office kitchen pigs and thieves

### → OPTION #1: Make a video

Nobody knows exactly who leaves dishes encrusted with dried tomato sauce on the counter. Buy a security camera and secretly tape the comings and goings of your coworkers in the kitchen. Then, once a week, hold a viewing party for all employees and humiliate the repeat offenders. Give them a special booby prize—a fresh sponge and dish soap.

### → OPTION #2: Set a trap

Rig a Lean Cuisine with those powder packets that banks use for stolen money. So when the fridge hijacker opens the frozen meal, it will explode all over him and everyone will know he's the thief.

### → OPTION #3: Organize a potluck lunch

To find out who keeps putting their half-eaten Lean Cuisine in the fridge for a week, put up flyers announcing a catered-in lunch. Those scavengers love free food so they'll all show up. But when they arrive, instead of seeing a lovely spread from the Green Door Café, they will find all of the spoiled leftovers from the kitchen refrigerator splayed out on the conference room table. Rotten fruit, rock-hard pizza, mold-infested Tupperware, sticky condiment packets, all of it. Lock the door and refuse to let anyone out until they claim their decaying dishes. Since the stench will be overwhelming, people will 'fess up quickly.

### → OPTION #4: Get revenge

Anyone who cooks smelly food at work should be killed, but since that's illegal, here's another solution. Plant fish scales and putrid cheese in hidden spots in the offender's work space. Eventually, they will be overwhelmed by the disgusting odor and, unable to find the source and get ride of it, will learn their lesson.

### OMGesus!

Are we working in sweatshops? 40 percent of employees say they don't take a real lunch break. Women are more likely to bring lunch from home and usually eat frozen entrees, fruit, salads, and soups, according to a study by the National Restaurant Association.

### The Five Worst Food Smells Coming Out of Office Kitchens

1. Popcorn
2. Burnt coffee
3. Indian food
4. Egg salad
5. Moldy sponges

It's bad enough that your superior is always ogling your bub-bies. But that's a dream compared to his other annoying habit. He's a close talker and, unfortunately, nobody—including you—has the balls to tell him that his breath could kill a dragon.

## The OMG! solution to dealing with a boss whose mouth smells like ass

### → OPTION #1: Offer everyone PepOMints

Bring a pack into a meeting and offer it to everyone, so he doesn't feel like you're referring to him only.

### → OPTION #2: Wear a surgical mask

Blame it on a fear of catching swine flu.

### → OPTION #3: Leave gifts

When you know he's out for lunch, sneak into his office and place dental floss and a tongue scraper on his desk.

### → OPTION #4: Give him an herb garden

Put parsley, tarragon, rosemary, mint, cloves, and fennel seed on his windowsill. Supposedly, chewing on these herbs helps mask bad breath. Carrots and apples also help, too.

### → OPTION #5: Send an anonymous message

Visit www.badbreathogram.com, which will send a discreet, humorous e-mail to the poor soul whose mouth smells like dirty feet.

**OMGeezus!**

More than 90 million Americans have bad breath.

### Celebrities with Dragon Breath

**Will Smith:** *According to Social-iteLife.com, an extra on* Hancock *says the star's breath smelled like "hot shit" and made his/her eyes water.*

**Ben Affleck:** *Sandra Bullock reportedly complained that her* Forces of Nature *co-star had stank mouth and gave him a tin of Altoids.*

**Hugh Grant:** *Rumors swirled that friends of the English star of* Music and Lyrics *begged him to chew on Listerine strips at the 2002 Academy Awards.*

**Julia Roberts:** *The actress had to apologize to her* Duplicity *costar Clive Owen because during kissing scenes her breath stunk from eating peanut butter sandwiches: "I'd say, 'Honey, do you have a mint?'"*

**Hitler:** *"He should have grown a beard to hide his mouth," his former secretary once said about his yellowing teeth.*

## In the Future...

- Don't eat a lot of onions and garlic or drink a lot of booze, coffee, or citrus drinks.
- Drink a lot of water. Dry mouth causes bad breath.
- Don't have an eating disorder. Dieters often can peel paint with their stinky fumes.
- Don't smoke.

**Dwight Yoakam:** *The country star's former lover Sharon Stone once said, "Kissing Dwight was like eating a dirt sandwich."*

**Clark Gable:** *He had excessively bad breath, his Gone with the Wind costar Vivien Leigh complained. "Kissing Clark Gable was not that exciting," she once said. "His dentures smelled something awful."*

# 84. You get drunk and make out with the mailroom guy at an office party

**W**henever he drops off your packages, the mailroom guy always flirts with you. He's totally cute, but you don't even know his name. So, fast-forward to the company picnic. It's 102 degrees outside and you've downed too many Rolling Rocks to keep hydrated. The next thing you know, the DJ puts on "Poker Face," your favorite song, and magically you are grinding with the mailroom guy—and shoving your tongue down his throat. You wake up the following morning and are mortified. You wish you didn't remember, that you had blacked out. No such luck. Every single moment is ingrained in your brain.

## The OMG! solution to downplaying a PDA at a corporate function

### →OPTION #1: Pretend he's your boyfriend

Elaine Benes did it on *Seinfeld*. After she hooked up with her coworker in front of everyone, she told everyone they were dating. If you're a couple, then kissing at an office party is not as shameful, although it is nauseating anyway.

### →OPTION #2: Secure your financial future

Go to the mailroom guy and tell him that you are going to file a sexual harassment suit, and that if he goes along with it, you can split the money and move to Tahiti. Together.

### → OPTION #3: Butter everyone up

Come in the next morning with a giant box of Dunkin' Donuts. Mmm, Munchkins.

*In the Future...*

Be more discreet. After everyone leaves work, the best places to do it are:

On the boss's desk

In an emergency exit stairwell

Against a file cabinet

In the backseat of your car in the garage

In an elevator

### → OPTION #4: Flog you!

Walk down the halls whipping yourself with a cat-o'-nine tails. Make sure pieces of flesh are ripped from your body so it's clear that you apologize for your behavior.

### → OPTION #5: Deflect attention

Gather a group around your cube and gossip about anyone who isn't there. Talk about how slutty Melissa's outfit was. Spill secrets that people told you drunkenly in confidence, like that your boss has to use Viagra or that Michael is gay.

## OMGesus!

Who cares about sexual harassment suits! Italian sexologist Serenella Salomoni has found that affairs at work actually make people more productive, happier, and energetic!

### Romance Is Rampant at Work

According to Vault.com's Office Romance Survey:

- 58 percent of workers have had an office romance.
- 39 percent have an office "husband" or "wife."
- 32 percent have fooled around actually in the office.
- 26 percent have met their spouse at work.
- 21 percent have had an affair with their boss.

You get drunk and make out with the mailroom guy at an office party **<** **OMG!** |

# 85. Your cubemate's excessive phone chatter is making your ears bleed

It's bad enough that you're packed like sardines into your office, which is a maze of snot-green cubicles. There's no privacy whatsoever. The tool who sits next to you is on his phone all day long. He has crying fights with his girlfriend, orders lunch for the entire office, and leaves cloying messages for his cats at home. He also has the most annoying ringtone in the history of mankind. Every time his phone rings, which is like every ten minutes, your ears are assaulted with "Who Let the Dogs Out." Something's gotta give or you're going to have a mental breakdown like Britney Spears and shave your head.

## The OMG! solution to tuning out a coworker

### → OPTION #1: Wear headphones

Fight fire with fire. Listening to music at work may signify to some that you're rude or a slacker, though. So be sure to look productive.

## → OPTION #2: Ask to be moved

Ask a manager for a seat change. However, be warned that with a new cubemate you run the risk that she'll be worse than the old guy. What if she douses herself in cheap perfume, hums incessantly, or eats cabbage at her desk?

## → OPTION #3: Rat on him

Send an anonymous message to management that he surfs the Internet all day and smokes pot in his car at lunch.

### OMGesus!

Less than 39 percent of workers under the age of twenty-five like their job, a study by The Conference Board says. Only 9 percent of workers like their job so much, they'd marry it, another dumb study by Harris Interactive for Taleo found.

## → OPTION #4: Have an affair with him

Once you've seduced him you have two options: You can persuade him to change his annoying habits or you can report the affair to HR, which will either get him fired or get him moved.

### In the Future...

Get a job in Montana, Idaho, Wyoming, Nevada, Utah, Colorado, Arizona, or New Mexico, the states where workers are the happiest with their jobs, says a survey by The Conference Board.

## Cubicle Etiquette 101

1. Don't decorate it like a dorm room or put collectibles on every inch of your space.
2. Keep your damn shoes on. Your feet stink!
3. Turn the volume down on your computer.
4. Don't reek like an ashtray from a hundred smoke breaks.
5. If you're sick, stay home! Don't be a martyr. Nobody wants your germs!

## *On-the-Job Complaining*

According to the National Opinion Research Center at the University of Chicago, here's a list of people who love and hate their jobs.

| LOVE THEIR JOBS | HATE THEIR JOBS |
| --- | --- |
| Priests | Gas station attendants |
| Butlers | Amusement park workers |
| Firefighters | Bartenders |
| Architects | Therapists |
| Mechanics | Roofers |

# 86. You're scared you're getting laid off

**W**ith the economy in the toilet, companies are cutting the fat. That means anybody who's useless—and you know who you are—is getting canned. But since the country is broke, even people who are productive are getting the old heave-ho. You don't think you're useless but you're getting weird signs from your boss that another round of the firing squad is coming. Oh no! You don't want to live in a tent city and stand in a soup line!

## The OMG! solution to keeping your head off the chopping block

### → OPTION #1: Be visible but quiet

Make your presence and ideas known but don't try too hard. People can smell desperation!

### → OPTION #2: Be indispensable

Volunteer for the crap jobs nobody wants to do.

### → OPTION #3: Be humble

Like the Mafia, don't be flashy. Don't drive a brand new BMW to work or wear expensive jewelry or clothes. The higher-ups might not think you need a job if it looks like you're doing okay. They'll get rid of you before someone who drives a Pinto and has kicks from Payless.

## → OPTION #4: Be flexible

If they want you to take a pay cut, consider it. It's better than working at McDonald's, which may be your only option.

### OMGesus!

People steal $50 billion of office supplies, such as pens, Post-it notes, highlighters, coffee, Sweet 'n Low, and toilet paper, every year, according to CareerBuilder.com!

### Signs you're getting axed

- There are closed-door meetings that don't include you.
- Your desk is moved to Siberia.
- The HR lady can't make eye contact with you.
- You have little to no responsibility.
- Nobody asks your opinion about anything.

### Recession-proof Jobs

Funeral director

Fast-food worker

Air traffic controller

Registered nurse

Teacher

Surgeon

Veterinarian

Detective

Substance abuse counselor

## Take This Job and Shove It

Match the celebrity with the menial labor gig they had before they were famous:

| | | | |
|---|---|---|---|
| 1. | Ellen DeGeneres | A. | Oyster shucker |
| 2. | Steve Carell | B. | Mailman |
| 3. | Jennifer Aniston | C. | Waitress |
| 4. | Amy Adams | D. | Hooters waitress |
| 5. | Gwen Stefani | E. | Dairy Queen janitor |
| 6. | Tom Cruise | F. | Paper boy |
| 7. | George Clooney | G. | Construction worker |
| 8. | Denzel Washington | H. | Barber |
| 9. | Johnny Depp | I. | Ballpoint pen salesman |
| 10. | Chris Rock | J. | Red Lobster waiter |

*Guess what? Ellen wanted to be an oyster shucker, Steve, a mailman, etc. 3 is C, 4 is D, etc. Shocking, huh?

# 87. You called in sick—and got caught

**Y**ou wake up one morning with a pounding hangover. There's no way in hell you can make it through the day, so you call your work supervisor and tell her you have food poisoning and won't be able to make it in. After sleeping until noon, you eat a grilled cheese and drink a Coke and miraculously feel better. So when your unemployed friend calls and says, "Let's go shoot some pool!" you're in. Your afternoon turns into evening and suddenly you're drunk again and bar-hopping. Unfortunately, while you're out, you bump into the office brownnose. No doubt she will tell your supervisor you do not have food poisoning but were partying. You must think fast.

## The OMG! solution to keeping a stool pigeon quiet

### → OPTION #1: Get her drunk

Like blackout drunk so she doesn't remember anything about the night before. When she passes out, shave her eyebrows and draw a Sharpie mustache on her. The next morning, she will look in the mirror and realize she can't go to work either and have to come up with an excuse. She will call you for advice and you will bond. Your secret will be safe.

### → OPTION #2: Bribe her

Offer to do her expense reports, or some other time-consuming task, for the next month.

### → OPTION #3: Lie

Tell her you were on the way to the hospital when you had to throw up. Your friend pulled over and you puked in this bar.

### → OPTION #4: Tell a sob story

Cry and say you need rehab but you can't afford to go because you don't want to lose your job. Say that you're in AA but fell off the wagon and you want to keep it confidential. But that you promise to get your life together. She will feel sympathy and will instantly become an enabler.

## OMGesus!

The most popular day to call in sick is Wednesday, a Career-Builder.com survey found. About 43 percent of workers call in sick when they feel fine and just want to get more rest or go to a doctor's appointment.

## The Five Dumbest Sick Day Excuses Ever

According to Career Builder.com:

- "I forgot I was getting married today."
- "My snake got out of its cage and I can't find it."
- "The ghosts in my house kept me up all night."
- "I flushed my keys down the toilet."
- "I had to help deliver a baby."

## 88. Your boss brings his bratty kids to work

It's not even Take Your Daughter to Work Day, but when your boss walks in the door with his children trailing behind, you know who's gonna end up being the office babysitter—you. Like you don't have enough to do, now you have to keep these rambunctious rugrats occupied for the next eight hours! And they have to like you. If they sense that you hate kids, they'll tell your boss and you'll get fired.

### The OMG! solution to entertaining the chief's children

#### → OPTION #1: Candy

Go trick-or-treating to every person's desk in the office. The kids will get a smorgasbord of goodies, from jars of candy on a desk to homemade banana bread that's been sitting on someone's credenza for a week. They'll also receive a nice assortment of mustard packets, plastic spoons and napkins.

#### → OPTION #2: The mail room

Go up there and let them crawl around in some giant boxes. Grab some plastic packing material and let them pop the bubble-wrap until it's all flattened or someone threatens to kill you.

#### → OPTION #3: Arts & crafts

If your office has an art department, ask a designer to make up a coloring book. Then grab some markers from the supply closet. That'll waste at least an hour.

### → OPTION #4: Build stuff

Give them all of the office supplies on your desk—the stapler, pencil holder, paper clips, paper bins, binders, push pins, all of it. Have them build a pretend city using all of the items.

### → OPTION #5: Cleaning

Kids love cleaning! Give them a mop and some sponges and let them go to town on that filthy kitchen (see #82).

## OMGesus!

40 percent of workers think their boss is lousy and 48 percent would fire them—but the feeling is mutual. Almost a quarter of all bosses badmouth their employees!

### Hell to the Chief

According to a study at Florida State University:

- 39 percent of workers said their supervisor failed to keep promises.
- 37 percent said their supervisor failed to give credit when due.
- 31 percent said their supervisor gave them the "silent treatment."
- 27 percent said their supervisor made negative comments about them to others.
- 23 percent said their supervisor blamed others to cover up mistakes.

*"If you go to a costume party at your boss's house, wouldn't you think a good costume would be to dress up like the boss's wife? Trust me, it's not."*

—JACK HANDEY

## 89. You are grossly underpaid

You work like a dog at your job but you still eat Top Ramen for dinner every night and have to put gas in your car in $5 increments. You know some of your colleagues are making more money than you because they always seem to be wearing new shoes and blow tons of money going out drinking every night. So how do you get some of that?

### The OMG! solution to demanding a raise

#### → STEP #1: Schedule a meeting

But not on a Monday, which research shows is a day for firings and general chaos. Also, you probably look and feel like a troll from partying all weekend. Fridays aren't good either—all anybody cares about on that day is getting the hell out of there for the weekend.

#### → STEP #2: Practice your speech

Don't go in there and just spew stuff off the top of your head like Rainman. And don't throw a pity party and call the Whaaaaambulance. Nobody cares that your rent check keeps bouncing or that there's a giant crack in your windshield that you can't get fixed because you're so po'.

### →STEP #3: Take a Xanax

You want to be relaxed and confident, don't you? Well, then don't go in there without a little help from a little friend.

### →STEP #4: Don't take no for an answer

If the boss says no way Jose, don't just give up. Make sure you get something better, even if it's just a better parking space. Otherwise, you'll look like a doormat.

## OMGjesus!

40 percent of us are so scared of asking for a raise, we'll never do it in our lifetimes! C'mon, grow a nutsack! Women still only earn seventy-seven cents for every dollar that a guy earns, from waitresses to CEOs. That extra twenty-three cents translates to a loss of $2 million over your lifetime if you get a law degree, an MD, or an MBA, according to WomensMedia.com.

### →STEP #5: Blow your raise in Vegas

If you do get a raise, celebrate with a trip to Sin City. Put the entire amount of your raise on black on the roulette wheel. If you win, you are so psyched. If you lose, well, it's back to Top Ramen.

### The Highest-Paying Careers and Their Average Salaries

Time for a career change! According to the Department of Labor:

**Surgeon:** *$181,000*

**Anesthesiologist:** *$174,610*

**OB/GYN:** *$174,610*

**Psychiatrist:** *$151,380*

**Airline Pilot:** *$134,090*

**Lawyer:** *$110,590*

**Astronomer:** *$96,780*

# 90. You send a nasty e-mail to the whole office

It's your worst nightmare. The lamest person in your office sends a mass e-mail asking everyone to buy her daughter's Girl Scout cookies. Instead of simply replying to your office BFF, you accidentally hit Reply All with this message: "We should buy a lot of Thin Mints so her little hobgoblin can finally fix that hair-lip! LOL!" Now everyone in the office thinks you're a heartless monster.

## The OMG! solution to sending a nasty e-mail

### → STEP #1: Apologize and empathize

Go to the cookie lady in person and say you're sorry and that your niece also has a cleft palate.

### → STEP #2: Take your checkbook out

And buy 100 boxes of Girl Scout cookies.

### → STEP #3: Consider Hara Kiri

This ancient Japanese ritual, in which a defeated samurai warrior would commit suicide by disem-boweling himself with a short knife, seems like an appropriate punishment.

## OMGesus!

A study by officebrokers.com in the U.K. found that forty-two e-mail mistakes are made every minute—60 percent of the e-mails were sent to the wrong person, 33 percent were raunchy, and 25 percent mocked the person it wasn't intended to go to.

;-D

## In the Future...

Learn proper e-mail etiquette. Don't be one of these douchebags:

- Don't just write "Thanks." It's assumed you're thankful. Nobody wants to go to the trouble of opening an e-mail and seeing one word.

- Never forward jokes. EVER.

- Don't list everyone you know on an e-mail. Create a list in your address book so people maintain some damn privacy.

- Write like an adult. Don't use text slang.

- No emoticons at work.

OMG!

# Chapter 10

# Party **Fouls**

## 91. Your guest arrives empty-handed

**Y**ou throw a fabulous party and when most people walk in the door, they give you a bottle of wine, a six-pack of beer, or at least some weed. But there's always one selfish bastard that walks in with nothing more than a shit-eating grin. Then he expects to drink all of your booze (and will probably leave the toilet seat up).

### The OMG! solution to getting rid of a freeloader

#### → OPTION #1: Call the cops

Bust up your own party. Then once the place is cleared out, secretly invite everyone else to come back.

#### → OPTION #2: Charge a cover

Ask for ten bucks and watch him split like an atom.

#### → OPTION #3: Be boring

Pretend you're having a book club meeting and watch him scurry like a roach in bright light.

## OMGesus!

The Top 10 Regifted Items, according to regiftable.com are:

1. Clothes
2. Housewares
3. Gift baskets
4. Picture frames
5. Jewelry
6. Cookbooks
7. Candles
8. Fruitcake
9. Gift cards
10. Booze

## In the Future...

The least anyone can do is regift! According to a poll by Harris Interactive for the Tassimo Hot Beverage System:

- 78 percent of Americans think it's okay to regift! Cheapskates!
- 77 percent regift because they think the gift is perfect for the other person.
- 30 percent have regifted gift cards or gift certificates.
- 29 percent recognized the regift because they were there when the gift was first given.
- 16 percent of regifters were spotted because the gift tag had the wrong name on it!

# 92. Someone hooks up a karaoke machine

**Y**ou wanted your shindig to be totally mellow, where everyone could just chillax. But then some dope brings a karaoke machine and all of a sudden it's like *American Idol* in your living room. Except everybody sounds more like Heidi Montag than Adam Lambert and people are picking the worst songs ever. It's ruining your party! You need to take control.

## The OMG! official list of karaoke song crowd pleasers

### → OPTION #1: Current hits

If your voice sounds like a cat in heat, stick to uptempo Top 40 hits to be safe. Everyone will join in, drowning out your headache-inducing warbling.

### → OPTION #2: Power ballads

If you actually have a decent voice, try the classic power ballads—they're always a crowd favorite. Some ideas are "Sweet Child O' Mine" by Guns N' Roses, "More Than Words" by Extreme, "Beautiful" by Christina Aguilera, "Sister Christian" by Night Ranger, and "Wanted Dead or Alive" by Bon Jovi are all acceptable.

### → OPTION #3: Oldies but goodies

Neil Diamond, Journey, Michael Jackson, Madonna (yeah, she's old), and Elvis always seem to make people happy for some reason. And everybody knows "Piano Man" by Billy Joel.

### → OPTION #4: Group numbers

Songs that are sure to have everyone singing alone include "Bohemian Rhapsody" by Queen, girl anthem "I Will Survive" by Donna Summer, "Love Shack" by the B52's, and "Paradise by the Dashboard Lights" by Meat Loaf.

> *"Anything that is too stupid to be spoken is sung."*
>
> —VOLTAIRE

### → OPTION #5: Duets

"No Air" by Jordan Sparks and girl-friend-beater Chris Brown, "Crazy in Love" by Beyonce and Jay-Z, "I Got You Babe" by Sonny and Cher, "Endless Love" by Lionel Richie and Diana Ross, and "Islands in the Stream" by Dolly Parton

and phone-sex and chicken lover Kenny Rogers.

## OMGesus!

People who sing in the car are safer drivers than mutes because it relaxes them, according to research by Privilege Insurance.

### The Ten Lamest Karaoke Songs

1. "Summer Nights" from Grease is like nails on a chalkboard.

2. "Lady Marmalade" is too hard to sing but groups of girls try anyway and end up screaming at the top of their lungs.

3. "I Will Always Love You" is headache-inducing.

4. Anything Japanese puts people to sleep.

5. Rap songs are just boring because it's all talking and nobody knows the words.

6. "Mony Mony" is just lame.

7. "The Electric Slide." It's self-explanatory.

8. Anything by Barry Manilow.

9. "Sweet Caroline" by Neil Diamond seems like a good idea until everyone screams, "So good! So good!" over and over and over.

10. "More than Words" by Extreme has difficult harmonies and nobody knows how to do it.

## 93. You catch peeps having sex on your bed

So you're having a party, and it's getting pretty wild. You need a moment's peace so you go into your bedroom. But when you get there, a couple is full-on having sex—on top of your favorite stuffed animals!

### The OMG! solution to dealing with fornication on your futon

#### → STEP #1: Coitus interruptus

Make your presence in the room known. Turn on the lights and clap your hands really loud.

#### → STEP #2: Gather their belongings

While they're startled like deer in the headlights, throw their clothes out the window.

#### → STEP #3: Make them do the Walk of Shame

If you want, give them washcloths to cover their privates. But if you don't feel like it, make them walk through your place, past all the partygoers, buck naked.

#### → STEP #4: Remove the bedspread, take it to the cleaners the next day and send them a bill.

Immediately put them in a fireplace or bonfire and burn them to a crisp.

→ **STEP #5: Sleep on the couch**

It'll probably take at least a few days before you want to lie down on your own bed again.

## OMGesus!

In a poll of Manhattan high school students by *New York* magazine, 16 percent admitted they've had sex on their parents' bed. Only 1 percent of their parents thought their kids had possibly done that.

**The Strangest Sex Laws on the Books**

**Ames, Iowa:** *A man can't take more than three swallows of beer while holding his wife in his arms in bed.*

**Bozeman, Montana:** *No sex in the front yard of a home after sundown—if nude.*

**Alexandria, Minnesota:** *If a man has garlic, onion, or sardine breath while having sex, his wife is allowed to order him to brush his teeth.*

**Connorsville, Wisconsin:** *Guys can't shoot guns while their lover is having an orgasm.*

**Willowdalecan, Oregon:** *Men can be fined for talking dirty during sex.*

# 94. Everyone always rummages through your medicine cabinet

**P**eople are so nosy! If you took a random poll, around 40 percent would admit that they look in people's medicine cabinets in the bathroom. And if you have a party, no doubt there will be at least a few people who look in there for drugs, mouthwash, Q-tips, KY, condoms . . . .Your guests are obviously going to have to pee (and perhaps poop). But you don't want anyone going through your stuff.

## The OMG! solution to stopping the snoopers

### →OPTION #1: Clear it out

Didja know that only 42 percent of us clean our medicine cabinets out regularly? Before the party, take everything out of so it looks like a hotel room bathroom. Leave the soap though so nobody passes on hepatitis.

### →OPTION #2: Set a booby trap

This was on *Candid Camera* or something once. Stack the medicine cabinet with marbles, then shut the door. So when the busybody opens it, they'll all come spilling out and you'll know exactly who the rude person is.

### →OPTION #3: Load it with fake stuff

Stock it with douches, foot fungus and hemorrhoid cream, giant maxi-pads, dentures, and Mylanta. The snoopers will be so shocked and disgusted, they'll never want to look again.

**Bathroom Facts That Will Blow You Away**

- Your computer keyboard and mouse, and telephone, are more infested with germs than toilet seats, according to a recent University of Arizona study.
- Americans use 433 million miles of toilet paper each year, which could stretch to the sun and back, notes the book *The Out-house Reader*.

- 46 percent of men say they always put the toilet seat down, says Bernice Kanner, author of the book *Are You Normal? Lies!*
- Before 1935, toothbrushes were often made with pig hair and toothpaste was made from ox hooves' ashes, eggshells, bark, and bones, according to Colgate Professional (*www.col-gateprofessional.com*)!
- Q-tips were invented in 1923 and were originally called "Baby Gays." Homophobes!
- In the old days, men used to make condoms out of dried animal intestines glued or stitched together.

# 95. Someone spills red wine on your carpet

**E**veryone's pretty tipsy, so you didn't want to open up the bottle of Cabernet. But then you ran out of booze and had no choice. Of course, Drunk Girl immediately sloshes her glass around and spills her wine all over your new white fuzzy carpet from West Elm. Emergency!

## The OMG! solution to getting the red out

### → OPTION #1: Club soda

The carbonation helps lift the stain. But don't rub, just blot.

### → OPTION #2: Salt

Prevents the stain from settling in. Pour it on while the stain is still wet, leave overnight, then vacuum the next day.

### → OPTION #3: White wine

If you have any left, this acts as a neutralizer.

### → OPTION #4: Laundry or dishwashing detergent

Apparently, cleaners like Shout or Dawn get it out.

### OMGesus!

People have been getting drunk on wine for 4,500 years! King Tut apparently preferred red wine over white, a study by Spanish researchers at the University of Barcelona and published in *Analytical Chemistry* has found.

## → OPTION #5: The dumpster

If it's a lost cause, dump it.

> "To alcohol . . .
> the cause of, and
> solution to, all of life's
> problems."
>
> —HOMER SIMPSON

### Rationalization Techniques . . .

. . . AKA "the health benefits of red wine":

- Wine increases the female sex drive.
- Men who drink less than half a glass of wine a day may live up to five years longer than men who don't drink anything at all.
- Obese mice that were given red wine lost weight without changing their diet, which was like eating McDonald's.
- Wine helps people do better in math.
- Wine helps prevent lung cancer, heart disease, high cholesterol, prostate cancer, E. coli infections, and damage from radiation exposure!
- Wine slows aging.

# 96. Your guests won't leave

Your party was a ton of fun but now it's 3:30 A.M. and you're ready for bed. You've been up since 6 A.M. preparing for this thing and you're exhausted. But when you start yawning nobody is getting the hint. One person even made coffee and is talking your ear off. How can you ask everyone to vamoose without being totally rude?

## The OMG! solution to kicking everyone out

### → STEP #1: Put on Pink Floyd

This granola, psychedelic band is a natural sedative. Once you put this on, your guests' eyes should glaze over.

### → STEP #2: Start cleaning up

Pick up all of the dirty dishes and empty bottles, which will make it clear that the end is near.

### → STEP #3: Put on your pajamas

Disappear for fifteen minutes and get ready for bed. Put on your most obvious sleeping clothes, like footie pajamas with Dora the Explorer all over them.

### → STEP #4: Brush your teeth

Leave the door open so everyone can hear you. Wash all of your makeup off and put a mouth guard or retainer in. When you come out of the bathroom, every-one will be so horrified by your appearance, they'll get the hint.

### → STEP #5: Bring out the photo albums

If that still doesn't work, make everyone look at your baby pic-tures, the most boring activity in the history of mankind.

### → STEP #6: Fall asleep in a chair

If all else fails, zonk out in front of everyone.

## OMGjesus!

The longest dance party in the world was held in India in 2004 and lasted fifty-five hours, accord-ing to the *Guinness Book of World Records*.

## In the Future...

Host a pre-party—according to the *Journal of American College Health*, 45 percent of all college drinking events involve a pre-party, and it will make everyone drunk and tired earlier.

> "Guests, like fish, begin to stink after three days."
>
> —BENJAMIN FRANKLIN

# 97. The food at a dinner party is revolting

Your friend who just moved into her new pad invites your group of friends over for a dinner party. She likes to think she's Rachel Ray, but, unfortunately, she's more like Ray Charles. She is blind to the fact that she can't cook. She gets an A for effort but an F for execution. Her food is bland and tasteless but you don't want to hurt her feelings.

## The OMG! list of excuses to avoid eating a mushy meal

### → OPTION #1: You're on a cleanse

It's all the rage to drink pepper water for nine days or whatever. Tell your hostess that you are on a liquid diet. Then drive thru Taco Bell on the way home.

### → OPTION #2: You have an eating disorder

Do things that anorexic people do so everyone thinks you have an issue with food. Like, put a laxative next to your water glass. Separate the food on your plate into weird piles and push them around. Disappear into the bathroom a few times.

### → OPTION #3: You're having surgery in the morning

You've been told by your doctor that you can't eat twelve hours before the procedure.

## → OPTION #4: You have IBS

Pull the hostess aside and tell her that you have just been diagnosed with irritable bowel syndrome and that everything you eat comes right out the other end. Until it's under control, you can't eat in public, fearing that you'll poop in your pants.

## → OPTION #5: Religious reasons

Mention that you're fasting for Ramadan. Nobody will ask questions because they will all be scared of you since you've converted to Islam.

### OMGjesus!

A California Air Resources Board study once found that preparing home-cooked meals by boiling, baking, roasting, and sautéing exposes us to dangerous pollutants and often violates indoor air standards!

> "I love Thanksgiving turkey . . . it's the only time in Los Angeles that you see natural breasts."
>
> —CALIFORNIA GOVERNOR ARNOLD SCHWARZENEGGER

### Kiss the Cook

- 78 percent of men think that cooking is a "sexy hobby" for women, a poll in *Grazia* magazine found.
- More men than women enjoy cooking, a *Taste of Home* survey says.
- 10 percent of wives admit their husbands are better cooks.
- 50 percent of Japanese men cook once a week, a survey from Nikkei Shimbun found.
- 57 percent of men cook at home and enjoy doing it, according to "The Great Male Survey" on AskMen.com.

# >>> 98. You have to vomit . . . at a frat party

**A** cute guy invites you to an Around the World party at Delta Doofus Omega. After you've drunk sake, tequila, Italian wine, and a couple of White Russians together, the room starts spinning like a merry-go-round. You are going to lose it for sure, but you don't want your date to lose respect for you if he thinks you're a lightweight. You really want to kiss him, but he won't if you have puke breath!

## The OMG! solution to sobering up

### → OPTION #1: Eat starch

Sneak into the roach-infested kitchen and find a loaf of bread or some stale crackers.

### → OPTION #2: Drink coffee

There's no scientific evidence that this will do anything, but mentally it helps.

### → OPTION #3: Cold shower

Ask to borrow your date's flip-flops first, though. You don't want to go into that petri dish of bacteria barefoot!

### → OPTION #4: Get slapped

Have a friend smack you across the face hard several times. Again, this doesn't technically do anything. But they do that in the movies and it seems to work.

## → OPTION#5: Exercise

Run around the block five times so the booze is sweated out of your pores.

## OMGesus!

30 percent of Americans have a drinking problem, according to a study in the *Archives of General Psychiatry*!

## In the Future...

Whatever you do, don't let a horny guy convince you to play drinking games. A study at Loyola Marymount University show that women get way more hammered than men during Quarters, Thumper, and Flip Cup!

### Beer Pong Drama

- When a state senator in Maryland tried to pass a bill outlawing beer pong, he got so many furious e-mails in protest, he withdrew the legislation.
- The National Institute of Health says drinking out of the same beer pong cups can spread herpes and E. coli!
- Joseph B. Jimenez, 24, was charged with first-degree murder for allegedly fatally shooting Scott Riley, 25, in Philadelphia after arguing over a game of beer pong.

### Best Cures for a Hangover

A shot of whiskey

Sleep

Fried egg sandwich with bacon

Spicy food

Having sex

Marijuana

Pickle juice

A gun

# 99. You accidentally take E

You're at a rave in a giant barn in the middle of nowhere. A weirdo wearing a trenchcoat and waving a glowstick overhears you say that the trance music and flashing lights are giving you a splitting headache. He tells you he has a magic pill to cure you, and he pops what you think is an aspirin in your mouth. But within fifteen minutes you feel funny. Oh no, you just swallowed Ecstasy!

## The OMG! solution to tripping out for the next six hours

### → STEP #1: Dance

You're rolling. You might as well take advantage of the high. Even if you are the worst dancer on the planet and you despise electronica, tonight you are like a contestant on *So You Think You Can Dance?*

### → STEP #2: Love everyone

Ecstasy will make you want to caress everyone you meet and be their best friend. You will spill your deepest darkest secrets but be accepted by everyone.

### → STEP #3: Eat a lollipop

All of your senses are heightened, including taste.

## → STEP #4: Stare

Since you'll have mental clarity like never before, observe the world around you with fresh eyes!

## → STEP #5: Don't die

People on E can overheat, damage their brain cells permanently, or drown from drinking too much water. They also get really depressed coming down.

### OMGesus!

Skip the E for something more organic. 79 percent of people who took magic mushrooms in a study by Johns Hopkins University reported being much happier with their lives two months later!

### Drugs—not hugs!

According to a report by the Substance Abuse and Mental Health Services Administration of Department of Health and Human Services:

- Rhode Island has the highest percentage of people doing drugs (12 percent); Texas has the lowest (6 percent).
- The top states for marijuana addiction are Rhode Island, Vermont, D.C., New Hampshire, and Alaska.
- The top states for cocaine addiction are D.C., Rhode Island, Arizona, Colorado, and Massachusetts.

### In the Future...

Know the druggie lingo before you pop anything in your mouth. Other names for E or X include B-bombs, disco biscuits, go, Scooby snacks, and sweeties.

# >>> 100. Your BFF's boyfriend hooks up with another girl at your place

**Y**our friend is out of town and can't make your party. Her boyfriend, however, shows up, gets drunk, and disappears into your bathroom with the town hussy. Everyone knows what happened. And now you're stuck in the position that if she finds out from someone else first, your friendship is pretty much over.

## The OMG! list of cowardly ways to break bad news

### →OPTION #1: Pass the buck

Just let someone else do it and plead ignorance if it comes back to you. Say you were so drunk you had absolutely no idea what was going on.

### →OPTION #2: Write an anonymous letter

Wear gloves though, in case her father or uncle is a cop and can get prints.

### →OPTION #3: E-mail it

It's so much easier than doing it in person or on the phone.

### →OPTION #4: Soften the blow

Say, "I have good news and bad news. The good news is that my party was so fun. The bad news is that Tina Cropodopolis gave Timmy a blow job in the bathroom."

## Breaking Bad News

If you do it in person, borrow these key phrases from doctors, who have to break bad news all the time:

*"We have an unpleasant surprise."*

*"Sorry, this is bad news. But don't worry—all is not lost."*

*"What have you already been told?"*

*"Do you want the big picture or every detail?"*

### OMGesus!

If you don't want to tell your friend, their bad karma will get them anyway. According to a study at Colorado State University, secret romantic relationships take a physical toll on your health!

# >>> 101. You cancel your own wedding

**Y**ou've ordered the most gorgeous flowers, picked out the perfect canapés, and booked the hottest DJ in town. But the day before the big day, you realize you hate your fiancé. In fact, every time you think of spending the rest of your life with him and his nose whistles, your breathing becomes labored, you get sweaty, and you almost faint. The good news is that you don't have to suffer through an eternity with this putz. You just have to grow some serious balls and be prepared to be hated by about 150 people. After you tell your fiancé, the vendors, and your parents you're not going through with it, do the following:

## The OMG! solution to bailing on your nuptials

### → STEP #1: Tell the guests

You're gonna have to call everyone. To avoid uncomfortable silences, homicidal threats, and weeping, call people at 4 A.M. and leave a message. Then, in the morning, change your number, dye your hair, and skip town.

### → STEP #2: Get rid of the dress

If it's custom made and you can't return it, you can try to sell it on eBay, give it to charity, or save it and wear it the following Halloween, when this will all blow over, and it'll be really hilarious and a great story to tell at parties.

### → STEP #3: Return the presents

Even if you already started using them, they have to go back. Well, maybe not that giant, chocolate-colored double-penetration dildo you got at your bachelorette party, but the KitchenAid mixer for sure.

### → STEP #4: Eat the cake

All of it. The sugar overdose will send you into a diabetic coma and then everyone will feel sorry for you instead of your ex-fiancé.

## OMGesus!

It's been widely reported that the average wedding now costs about $27,000, roughly the same price as a letter written by Princess Diana, a new Mustang, or the recent bar tab for the Pussycat Dolls.

### The Three Best Destinations for Runaway Brides

1. North Korea or Namibia. They have no extradition deals with the United States.
2. All Gay Nude Male Windjammer Caribbean Cruise. You get the feel of a Caribbean honeymoon with stops including St. Barts, Antigua, and St. Maarten, with the guarantee that you won't be bothered by any men.
3. Queens. New York City has 8 million people and you can blend right into this borough. As Atlanta Braves pitcher John Rocker once noted, Queens is chock full of "neanderthals" and "degenerates," which now you are because you did something really despicable.

Congratulations! Now you know how to handle all of life's most f'ed situations. There is a plane ticket to Iraq waiting for you at the counter of the airport. Good luck and OMGodspeed!

# Acknowledgments and Apologies

I'd like to first and foremost thank my amazing parents, John and Linda Baer, for their unconditional love and support. You are my rock. Also, my agent Molly Lyons at Joelle Delbourgo Associates and my editor Chelsea King at Adams Media. Big shout out to my brilliant yet bananas family at *In Touch* magazine, including but not limited to: Jaime, Liza, Paola, Melvin, Graves, Snowball, Rachie, Sully, and my young muses Kara and Gina. I'd like to thank hot dogs for existing, The Thompson LES and meerkats, Brett and Cathy for encouraging me to become a writer, the Academy, Buster and Benihana, my shrink Gerri, beer in a can, the Chicago White Sox, EJ and Vix, Brad Pitt, Angelina Jolie, Suri Cruise, and Jon Gosselin for ensuring I kept my job during the recession, the cast of *Mad Men* for being so hot, Sophie, my dead birds Tiki and Punky RIP, $5 footlongs, Chaz Bono, Crew Pomade, white tube socks, porn on cable,

New York City, and Stuart, the guy behind the counter at Shake Shack, who makes my cheese fries. Actually, it could be Stewart. I didn't ask.

I'd like to apologize to Pam and Steve Adelman. They sent me a singing telegram after I had surgery in junior high and I never sent them a thank-you card. I've been carrying that guilt around for thirty years. I'll take this opportunity to say sorry to my Jeep for abandoning it in Fort Lee, to Brad, Angelina, and Suri Cruise (but not Jon Gosselin) for making your life a living hell, to my lungs for all that cigarette smoke, to all those people I've flipped off in my car because of clinical road rage, to all the people who hate me because I love Sarah Palin, to all the beautiful women who haven't had the opportunity to date me, including Sarah Palin, to Benihana for all those times I lied and said it was my birthday and got free green tea ice cream, and to my geology professor in college—it was really rude of me to fall asleep sitting in the first row during your lectures.

# About the Author

Deborah Baer is a Brooklyn-based entertainment writer and editor. Over the last thirteen years, she has worked for publications such as *In Touch*, *CosmoGirl!*, *Lifetime*, *Parents*, *Ladies' Home Journal*, and the *New York Daily News*. She has profiled many big, fancy celebrities, including Mariah Carey, Angelina Jolie, Katie Holmes, Ellen DeGeneres, Lindsay Lohan, and Britney Spears (who would probably never even think of mentioning Deborah in their bios). She has also coauthored two political humor books, *Blue v. Red* and *Red v. Blue*, about the 2004 presidential election. So, with all of this mind-blowing success, why is she still broke? It doesn't make any sense.

# Art Credits

tuna © iStockphoto/Karimala
plane © iStockphoto/luminis
bird poo © iStockphoto/crazydevilmouse
lotto balls © iStockphoto/Marina_Ph
legs © iStockphoto/double_p
black cat © iStockphoto/GlobalP
nametag © iStockphoto/rodmacpherson
dog © iStockphoto/Pumba1
woman in towel © iStockphoto/fotek
drink © iStockphoto/pixhook
fist © iStockphoto/arakonyunus
guido © iStockphoto/1001nights
stripper © iStockphoto/4x6
whoopee cushion ©
    iStockphoto/Joe_Potato
gym man © Simone van den Berg/123RF
lesbians © FotoSearch/Image Source
dumbbells © iStockphoto/pkruger
recorder © iStockphoto/Renphoto
cell phone © iStockphoto/daboost
breakfast © iStockphoto/pixhook
camera © iStockphoto/jaroon
burger © iStockphoto/anopdesignstock
joystick © iStockphoto/shmackyshmack
biting underwear ©
    FotoSearch/Image Source
tombstone © iStockphoto/clintspencer
ketchup © iStockphoto/tacojim
dirty pots © iStockphoto/tap10
toy train © iStockphoto/mammamaart
broken heart © iStockphoto/DNY59
rosary beads ©
    iStockphoto/PaulMaguire
tampon © iStockphoto/Floortje
snake © iStockphoto/texcroc

credit card © iStockphoto/farelka
clown © iStockphoto/sdominick
middle finger © iStockphoto/1001nights
pregnancy test © iStockphoto/evemilla
shopping cart © NeubauWelt
broken vase © iStockphoto/marylooo
scrunchies ©
    iStockphoto/Sweetymommy
VIP © iStockphoto/fotografstockholm
magnifying glass © iStockphoto/Edin
disco ball © iStockphoto/deliormanli
sexy photo © FotoSearch/Image Source
mom pic © iStockphoto/jashlock
slippers © iStockphoto/RuslanDashinsky
laptop © iStockphoto/CostinT
stethoscope © iStockphoto/dulezidar
poop © iStockphoto/LPETTET
popcorn © iStockphoto/jmb_studio
fish © iStockphoto/shem
gum © iStockphoto/jjauregui
cigarette butt ©
    iStockphoto/darklord_71
donuts © iStockphoto/Maliketh
earphones © iStockphoto/Dizzy
axe © iStockphoto/majkel
fruitcake ©
    iStockphoto/sumnergraphicsinc
microphone © iStockphoto/kevinruss
garlic © iStockphoto/timsa
dentures © iStockphoto/HansUntch
red wine © iStockphoto/Mattjeacock
fish background © iStockphoto/Sieto
pill © iStockphoto/prosado
whisper © FotoSearch/Image Source
runaway bride © iStockphoto/A-Digit